To Be Somebody

Beverly Boone • *Nate Lowe*

To Be Somebody

Copyright © 2007 Beverly Boone and Nate Lowe. All rights reserved. No part of this book may be reproduced or retransmitted in any form or by any means without the written permission of the publisher.

Published by Wheatmark®
610 East Delano Street, Suite 104
Tucson, Arizona 85705 U.S.A.
www.wheatmark.com

Publisher's Cataloging-In-Publication Data
(Prepared by The Donohue Group, Inc.)

Boone, Beverly.
  To be somebody / Beverly Boone and Nate Lowe.

  p. : ill. ; cm.

  ISBN-13: 978-1-58736-722-9
  ISBN-10: 1-58736-722-X

  1. Lowe, Nate—Childhood and youth. 2. African Americans—Biography. 3. African Americans—Mississippi—Biography. 4. Children of sharecroppers—Mississippi—Biography. 5. Psychologists—Biography. I. Lowe, Nate. II. Title.

CT275.L69 B66 2007
976.206/3/0922006935575

All the events depicted herein are true, but some names have been changed to protect the privacy of certain individuals.

In memory of my mother
Willie B Lowe.
May you rest in peace forever more.

In memory of my "play" mother
Mrs. Mathilda Griffin,
A cornerstone of my life

In memory of Mr. Sylvester Alford,
My mentor and role model

Dedicated to the memory of Edward MacDonald,
A dear friend and beautiful soul to whom we owe so much.
We remember you with love and gratitude.

Contents

Acknowledgments..ix
Chapter One...1
Chapter Two...10
Chapter Three...19
Chapter Four..31
Chapter Five..38
Chapter Six...44
Chapter Seven...51
Chapter Eight...60
Chapter Nine..69
Chapter Ten...76
Chapter Eleven..84
Chapter Twelve..95
Chapter Thirteen...101
Chapter Fourteen...108
Chapter Fifteen..115
Chapter Sixteen..122
Chapter Seventeen..129
Chapter Eighteen...138
Chapter Nineteen...145
Chapter Twenty...153
Chapter Twenty-one...161
Chapter Twenty-two...167
Chapter Twenty-three...172
Chapter Twenty-four..180

Acknowledgments

There is no way this manuscript could have been written without the help and encouragement of key people in my life. To each one of you I say, thank you from the bottom of my heart. I am honored to have shared my life with you. To my family, Joann, Sharon, Sharnell, Sha'von and Sharine—-you're the greatest. Lionel P. Jenkins (Chip), my high school pal, thanks for your friendship. Jamison Davis (Sugar Bear), my college friend, you came through for me when I really needed you. I will never forget you, Mr. Henry Redmond, my high school football coach, I was so inspired by your prayer before every game. Mr. A. T. Williams, my high school principal, you made a real difference in my life. Mrs. A. T. Williams, my high school English teacher, thanks for challenging me to be the very best I could be. Dr. Stan Hatkoff, my commanding officer, thanks for your understanding, consideration, and friendship.

Thanks to Reverend Roberta Catlett for your support kindness and genuineness. You are special. Ms. Beverly Boone, the co-author of this book, you provided the missing link to making this book a reality. Your hard work, dedication, commitment and steadfastness paid off.

Finally, thanks to all of you who insisted that I write this book to illustrate and demonstrate that it's not where you come from in life. It doesn't matter what people think of you. What matters is what you think of yourself and where you are headed. With the right attitude and spirit there is no limit to what you can achieve.

—Dr. Nate Lowe

Chapter One

There was no doubt. She was pregnant. Her belly bulged against the stiff cotton of her flowered work dress. The bulky aprons she wore to work at Miss Ann's were beginning to fail to hide what she had suspected. Soon Big Mama would know. Soon everyone would know.

But Willie B felt no shame. She sat on a wooden chair in Big Mama's kitchen waiting for her loaves to finish baking. It was a crisp late spring Sunday morning. Big Mama garbed in her stiff white and blue polka dot dress, white gloves, white purse and white hat, left early for church. Willie came over as usual to do Mama's chores and baking and look after Paw Paw while she was gone. Willie got up and looked out the screen door to check on Emanual, her second son, all of six years old.

She remembered holding him in her arms when he was just a baby. A chill ran up her spine when she first noticed how he looked at her as through his colicky tears. His soft brown eyes strained as though he expected she might disappear. His crying would increase and Willie B could do little to calm him. "Don't you worry my precious boy. Mama loves you. Mama's not goin' nowhere," she'd whisper into his tiny ear.

Emanual looked up from the tin can fort he was building in the yard. He smiled and waved at his mother. She waved back and grinned. "Always lookin' for his Mama," she said to herself.

Life was soon going to get better for her, Manual, Teenie, and the baby she was carrying. Willie B could feel it deep down in her heart. "Nathaniel will be so happy. I just know it," she told herself. He would marry her and they'd all be a family. Nathaniel, himself an orphan would certainly not turn his back on his own child.

She twirled one of the thick black plaits she wore on top of her head. The smell of the loaves baking warmed her nostrils. Paw Paw called from the back porch, but she didn't hear him. The old cloth mop stood in the bucket, the green and yellow linoleum waited to be scrubbed. In the yard, Big Mama's dresses and Paw Paw's shirts flapped feverishly in the wind. Paw Paw's brown plaid shirt pulled loose from its pins and tumbled around the grass as Manual played nearby.

Nathaniel would marry her. Mr. Charlie would give them a bigger house and plot of land. With Nathaniel, Manual and Teenie, her almost 15-year-old son, to work the cotton, they'd make so much money at picking time. And at the end of the season, Mr. Charlie'd pay them a bonus. A bonus for the first time ever. Fried chicken on the table on Sunday and new shoes for the whole family at Christmas. How wonderful life will be… She could see it all in her mind.

Baby boy so beautiful toddles at her feet as she arranges a pink and purple bouquet of flowers in a cup on the kitchen table. She smiles as baby tries to form his first words. "Is that fried chicken I smell, Honey?" Nathaniel comes into the kitchen just back from his day at Mr. Charlie's sawmill. He grabs Willie around the waist and plants a big kiss on her cheek as she flips a plump chicken leg in the grease. "And how's my little man?" Her husband picks up his son and holds him in the air. Little Nathaniel laughs and laughs. Willie B smiles. "He sure loves his Daddy."

"Oh Lord Almighty," Willie B gasped as the smell of burning bread reached her day dreaming mind. She pulled open the oven door with a kitchen rag and was in such a hurry she burned her hand on the bread pan. Sure enough the tops of the loaves had begun to turn black. "Oh Lord," she fretted, "Mama's gonna skin me alive when she gets home."

"Willie, Willie, where the hell are you?" Paw Paw shouted from the porch. Paw Paw, Cleve McDaniel was not Willie B's father. He was Big Mama's third husband. Another drunk, good for nothing.

She quickly walked Paw Paw inside. He was too drunk to make

it on his own. "God damn it," he slurred, "I done been callin' you for an hour, bitch."

"Please don't tell Mama," she begged.

But he was sure to ignore her plea. Of course he would tell his wife. Something good to talk about. Willie wasn't his daughter and he felt no loyalty to her.

Willie B's father died when she was just a girl. He was blind and needed a lot of tending. Since Big Mama didn't have the time to care for her first husband, Willie B stopped going to school in the third grade to stay home and tend to him while Big Mama worked in the fields. Willie never learned to read or write or even count. She wasn't very bright to begin with and her lack of schooling left her at a severe disadvantage. Big Mama always said that girls didn't need book learning.

"Paw Paw, please don't tell Mama," she begged again.

"Mind your tongue, girl and get me some of that corn whiskey," Paw Paw said. He raised his cane in the air as if to strike her. Ordering Willie around made him feel like he was somebody. She was the only one in his world that occupied a lower position than he.

Willie raced to do his bidding. Once he was situated with his whiskey in hand, she hurriedly scraped some of the black from the bread tops and bottoms and let the loaves sit out to cool. She picked up the mop and scrubbed down the floor. Big Mama would be so angry, but it seemed she was always upset with her daughter. Willie could never please her.

As she plunged the mop into the lye water, she laughed. "Just you wait, Mama. Just you wait, Paw Paw. Things is gonna be different round here real soon."

Willie B and her sons lived about an eighth of a mile up the road from Big Mama. In the hierarchy of sharecroppers on Mr. Charlie's plantation, Willie's family shack ranked so low they were given the smallest and most broken down of all Mr. Charlie's worker's shacks. Only Mr. Curly, an old man, too elderly to work anymore, who lived in a lean-to in the middle of the cow pasture, had it worse. The more money a sharecropper family made raising and picking cotton for Mr. Charlie, the better the house he provided. Large families with lots of children and many hands to do the picking got the best and largest houses and plots of land to work. Cousin Andrew and his thirteen children had a four-room house in the back of the field.

Willie prayed her baby would grow up to be a good cotton picker and improve the family's lot. Maybe she and Nathaniel would have more children, too. She had always been poor at picking cotton. Her hands were slow and her skin cracked and brittle from housework and milking cows morning and evening at Miss Ann's and at Big Mama's on the weekends. Her knuckles and fingers often bloody, her hands lacking dexterity, she most often dragged her cotton sack from the field with less than half the bolls the others had picked.

Manual showed little interest in picking cotton, preferring instead to dance around the turnrows and chase a butterfly or a bird here or there. Willie B didn't have the heart to scold him. He so loved and depended on her. As long as his Mama was where he could see her, he always wore a timid smile and had not a care in the world.

Otis, whom Willie nicknamed Teenie, was nearing manhood, but his behavior was far from maturing. He lived to run around with plantation women, drink and play music at local juke house. He was a wild young man who brought much heartache and disappointment to his Mama. About the only thing he liked more than chasing women was getting drunk and brawling. He was arrested several times, but Mr. Charlie always went and got him out of jail. Mr. Charlie's white friends on the police force knew he needed his man back to work as soon as possible, so when Mr. Charlie asked they dropped the charges. After Mr. Charlie dropped off her son, he hurled a string of insults and obscenities at Willie B., blaming her for Teenie's lack of acceptable behavior. Willie longed for Teenie to straighten up and be the man of her family. No matter how many times he got into trouble, no matter how bad the trouble was, she invariably forgave and loved her eldest son. She believed in her heart that he would change one day and make all their lives better.

Willie's wooden shack had two rooms—one for sleeping, the other for eating. Water had to be carried from the lake that flowed along the edge of the plantation. Whatever scarce wood they could gather provided heat in the winter, and the family burned coal oil lamps for lighting at night. There was no electricity or indoor plumbing.

The floors in the house were earthen. There was very little furniture—a couple of wooden benches and a small wooden table. In the sleeping room placed on rusted iron springs were a couple of stir mattresses, hand sown burlap sack casings filled with cotton bolls that had to be periodically stirred to make them puff up. The kitchen had a window with a cracked glass pane. A wood-burning stove dominated one side of the eating room. Dishes, laundry, and infrequent bathing were done in a #3 aluminum washtub.

After returning home from her Saturday work at Big Mama's, Willie B sat on a stir mattress, her head brimming with anticipation. Tonight was the night she planned to tell Nathaniel her wonderful news. He was coming by her house at six. She was excited and a little nervous, praying she'd find the right words to tell him. All her life the noise around her drowned out her tiny voice. Big Mama was always berating her, telling her she'd done wrong before she made a move, criticizing her cooking, her cleaning, her choices in men. Mr. Charlie's nasal voice was barking orders or insults at her. Paw Paw told her to shut up at least five times a day. No one wanted to hear what Willie B had to say. "Don't speak unless you got something to talk about," her Mama constantly told her. "Now I got somethin' wonderful to say," Willie announced to herself. She straightened her hair plaits and smoothed the skirt of her best-flowered cotton dress. With a soapy rag she dabbed at some dirt blotches near the hem. The road was muddy from a spring rain two nights ago, and she stepped in a puddle on her way back from dropping Emanual at Big Mama's. She took the glass stopper from a blue bottle of Evening in Paris and dabbed the pungent toilet water behind her ears and on her throat. Picking up her sweater, she went out on the porch and waited for her man to arrive.

About an hour later, Nathaniel strolled up to the house. He was late as usual, but she didn't care. She was so happy to see him and nearly bursting to tell him her news.

"Hello, Baby," Nathaniel said in his powerful baritone voice.

He was a handsome man with dark skin and eyes that pierced right through her.

"Hi, Nathaniel," she answered sheepishly. She couldn't look him in the eyes, but she couldn't look away. He was so beautiful, tall, and strong. Willie just knew her son would look just like him.

"Sorry I'm late, Baby."

"That's all right."

There was a silence. Willie was suddenly afraid and tongue-tied. She felt like she couldn't move and just sat there on the stoop gazing up at him.

"Come on, woman. Get over here and give me some sugar." She obeyed and as their lips met she relaxed.

"Let's go on inside. I don't feel like goin' to the juke house no more now that I see how good you lookin' tonight."

Willie nearly blushed and walked into the house with Nathaniel following close behind. She turned to say something and he was right in front of her, inches away. "Woman, you lookin' so good." He ran his hands along her waist around to the small part of her back and pulled her close. He chuckled. "I think you're puttin' on some pounds, Baby."

She looked up at him. Her eyes were wide with anticipation. "Yes, I am."

Nathaniel watched her, puzzled by the look on her face. He had seen that look before on a woman and it told him things were getting a bit too serious for his liking.

"I am gaining weight."

He laughed nervously. "I can feel that," he said, wishing he hadn't brought it up.

"Nathaniel, there's a reason." She trailed off.

"You're gonna have to explain."

"I'm carrying our child." She was nearly breathless after she said the words.

The smile vanished from Nathaniel's face. "I don't' know what net you got caught in, but I aint the Daddy."

"But you are," Willie gasped. She felt like the walls of the house were crumbling down around her.

"No I aint and I don't wanna hear you say I am. Don't be trying to pin this on me."

"But, Nathaniel, it is your baby."

"Don't you say that ever again," he shouted at her. He pulled away and she lost her balance falling against the wall. "It aint mine. Leave me the hell alone."

Nathaniel left that night. He barely spoke to her again. When the gossip loving plantation folk asked, he continued to deny Willie and his child. She was alone again. The baby she carried seemed more like a curse. The happiness she dreamed of was gone. Soon she'd have another mouth to feed, another soul to care for when no one cared for her. She secretly wished she'd miscarry.

The month dragged slowly on. Willie's stomach swelled so big that Big Mama swore she was carrying twins. It felt more like triplets. Working became increasingly difficult. When Christmas time arrived, Willie was summoned to her annual settlement meeting with Mr. Charlie. As she sat in his office on the side of the plantation store waiting for him to arrive, she fretted over the poor showing she had made that year. Her family was far under its cotton quota. Surely, she would owe money to Mr. Charlie. There was no point in even thinking about a settlement. Already up to her tab limit at the plantation store, she now would owe even more. Willie wiped her forehead with a red cotton rag and wondered how she could feed her boys through the long winter ahead. And soon the baby would come. She had no idea how they would all survive.

Mr. Charlie walked through the office door, his elder son Elm following close behind. He was a short man with a thin frame. He appeared wizened with piercing blue eyes, a broad forehead, thin lips and a wide nose. He wore his customary khaki pants that appeared two sizes too large and a white see through nylon shirt with a white under shirt. On his head was a straw hat with a green plastic sun visor inserted in the brim. Puffing at the butt of a thick brown cigar, he sat down at his desk.

"Evening, sir," Willie said, forcing a smile.

Rustling through a pile of yellow notepaper, Mr. Charlie ignored her greeting. Elm reached over his father's shoulder and pulled out the page with Willie's name printed on the top in bold black letters.

"All right, all right, I see it. Now leave me be," Mr. Charlie snapped at his son. Elm stepped back behind his father's chair.

"Evening, Mr. Elm," Willie B nearly whispered as she caught his eye.

"Evening, Willie B," Elm answered. Although his father's son, he felt sympathy for the sharecroppers, often disagreeing with his father's treatment of them. Oftentimes after Mr. Charlie had gone away following a tirade he would tell the workers, "Don't pay him no mind." Willie could see by the look in his eyes, he felt sorry for her now.

"Willie B Lowe, Willie B Lowe," Mr. Charlie repeated her name in his nasal tones, seeming to mock her.

"Yes, sir, Mr. Charlie?"

"You are the most good for nothin' nigger on my land. This year even worse than the last. I didn't think that was possible." He took his handkerchief from his pants pocket and blew his nose. After he finished he made a sharp snorting sound through his nostrils, two, three, four times before continuing. "What am I gonna do with you? I'm stuck taking care of you for the rest of your natural life, aint I?" he continued in his shrill lower class Southern accent. "I give you a roof over your sorry head, land to make a living, credit at my store, and I get next to nothin' from you." He banged a freckled white fist on the desk. "What am I gonna do with you and your good for nothin' bastard children?"

Willie could barely speak from fear. "I'm sorry, Mr.. Charlie, sir."

"Shut up, nigger. I don't want to hear your falsehoods. Your settlement for the year 1945 is you owe me $30 for the use of my land and dwelling."

"Yes, sir. Thank you, sir." Willie rose from her chair to leave. Her knees were shaking. She paused for a moment, wanting to say something, to promise to do better, to apologize for disappointing him again and doing him wrong again, but the words would not come.

"Go on, nigger. Get out of my sight," Mr. Charlie told her, his voice rising with frustration.

As she left the office, she felt her baby sharply kick her side. Her knees almost buckled, but she managed to get out the door.

The labor pains began late in the evening on January 25. Ma Pearl, Pearlie Morris, the plantation midwife, was summoned to assist with the birth. Ma Pearl, who lived on the neighboring Stein's plantation, was like the great mother of the plantations. Not only did she help with countless births, she had seven children of her own, provided daycare of sorts for many plantation parents, and had adopted several stray children. One baby boy she raised was brought to her after being found abandoned in a cardboard box by the side of the road. That child grew up and flourished under her care. He was Nathaniel, the father of Willie's baby. Ma Pearl was well aware her son denied being the father, but she felt no awkwardness toward Willie. She was there to help her and make five or ten dollars for her efforts.

Willie needed to rely heavily on all of Ma Pearl's knowledge and experience birthing babies. Her labor was long and excruciating. She screamed and cried and pushed for hours and hours. Ma Pearl feared Willie's heart might give out so difficult was the labor. During the hours of struggle and strain and knot arose in the middle of Willie's forehead. It remained for the rest of her life.

Finally, on January 26, 1946, she gave birth to a 13.5-pound boy. Upon seeing the child, Ma Pearl declared, "He's Nathaniel's son, all right. He looks just like his Daddy."

Willie B smiled and felt somewhat vindicated that Nathaniel's mother had recognized her child's paternity. She named the child. Nathaniel Lowe, taking his first name from his father as was the custom on the plantation when the mother was not married to the baby's father.

Chapter Two

The first couple years of Nate's life passed quickly. Because his mother had to work nearly ten hours a day, he spent much of his time being watched by his brother Manual, Big Mama or his paternal grandmother Ma Pearl. When Mama worked in the field and no one else could watch him, she placed him on a cotton sack ahead of her between two rows while she picked cotton nearby. As she moved up the row, she slid the cotton sack along the dirt so that Nate would always be in front of her where she could keep an eye on him. At the end of the day, Mama had almost no energy to care for her baby. What little she had left was divided with looking after Manual and cleaning up Teenie's messes.

Nate was just two years old when he first saw Mama in anguish. At that time her second son Emanuel was a young lad of six years. Emanuel had been conceived during a brief affair. There was no thought of marriage. The older Emanuel drove a log truck at the plantation sawmill and had his share of women. By the time Mama realized she was pregnant, he had little interest in her or her unborn child, and Willie was well aware of this fact. She spent no time fantasizing about a future with him. Before their son was born, he had moved on and was seeing a woman named Flora. The relationship was a serious one.

Nevertheless, he did visit his infant son a few times and never denied him, as Nate's father would later do. Soon, however, he and Flora left the plantation for a better life up north in Chicago. The couple married shortly after they moved.

Seven years passed before Emanual Sr. returned to the plantation to visit his parents. He very much wanted to see his namesake, too, and stopped by Mama's house.

Willie held no ill will against her former lover and welcomed him into her home. She listened as he boasted that he and Flora were expecting their first child. She felt happy for his good fortune. She beamed with pride as he marveled at his handsome son. So bright he was, and so well mannered. She absorbed his flattery and felt, special, even important. She had done well raising their boy. When it came time for him to leave, Emanual embraced his son and kissed him on the forehead. "I'll see you again soon, my little boy."

Willie B picked up her son and stood on the porch with him in her arms. The two waved good-bye until Emanual Sr. had disappeared from view.

The next morning she dressed quickly and headed to work at the big house, leaving Manual to watch little Nate. When she returned to check on the boys before going into the field, she found Nate alone and wailing in the middle of the sleeping room. Manual was nowhere to be found. She screamed, grabbed Nate, and ran frantically from house to house. She soon discovered that Emanual Sr. had left for Chicago and taken their son with him. She was heartbroken and inconsolable.

One day a week or so after the abduction, Mama with Nate in her arms was walking back from the field when she came upon Miss Pat. Always gossiping and in everyone's business, Miss Pat had never married and lived with another old woman named Miss Cheney in a small shack on the plantation.

"Afternoon."

"Afternoon, Willie B. Oh, look at that boy. He's sure growin' fast."

"Yes, he is, but he was a big one when he was born," Mama laughed.

"Child, aint you scared for him?"

Mama started. "Miss Pat, why you say that?"

Miss Pat clenched her toothless jaws, feigning reluctance to speak, but of course she couldn't wait to tell. " I'd be real careful with him, you hear? I think his Daddy's gonna come and snatch him just like Manual's Daddy did."

"Miss Pat, don't say such a thing, please." She quickly excused herself and ran all the way home, holding Nate close to her chest.

For years after, Mama was hyper-vigilant of Nate, fearing that at anytime Miss Pat's warning might come true. She lived her life constantly looking over her shoulder, always afraid to leave her child out of her sight.

In 1949, a terrible storm struck the plantation. There was no warning for the sharecroppers. Mama was terrified when the winds began to howl, and she picked up Nate and rushed over to her mother's house. Big Mama was scared of lightening and thunder, and Mama always stayed with her during a storm. This time Mama joined her mother to assuage her own fright. There was something unnatural about this storm. The winds grew stronger and stronger; the thunder louder and louder. The lightening seemed to be cracking right over their heads. Rain and hail pelted the roof. Mama could not help feeling this storm was bringing bad luck to the plantation. Powerful change was blowing in on the heels of the storm. Mama just knew it.

Mama huddled in the corner, hugging her boy close to her. Nate cried and cried. The awful noises frightened him, but he also felt his mother's fear. He wished he could take it all away and make her smile again. No one spoke as Big Mama scurried around the house hanging bed sheets on all the windows and mirrors. She believed that would keep the lightening out of the house.

Across the plantation lived an old widowed woman named Ma Sue. She was no more than four feet tall and had no teeth, but she could eat meat with the best of them. Mama felt sorry for Ma Sue and often took Nate to her one room shack to visit. Ma Sue made Nate a stack of flapjacks and smothered them with Brer Rabbit Maple Syrup. The hungry little boy whose Mama could not afford enough food, devoured the stack, savoring every sweet bite. Ma Sue marveled at his healthy appetite. Nate grew very fond of her.

Ma Sue was a God fearing woman. During the storm she sat on her wooden rocking chair and prayed to God to spare her and the people of the plantation. She sang hymns praising Jesus' name as the winds whistled through crack in the walls. Suddenly, a huge gust battered the shack. The roof ripped off. Ma Sue got under the kitchen table. When the men came after the storm had passed, they found her still under that table. She had never stopped praying.

People called her survival a miracle from God. She quickly became a legend. The local newspaper came and interviewed her. Folks said the plantation was spared because of the faith of Ma Sue.

The plantation was spared. Life began to turn back to normal. Mama tried to cling to the hope that Ma Sue's victory meant good things were ahead for all, but she knew deep down bad things were coming. She went back to working day in and day out. Some days she forgot the constant fear that her son would be stolen from her. Some days she barely noticed Nate, but some days she watched him incessantly, fearing he might be gone at any moment. It was confusing for the young boy. For a time Mama convinced herself that Ma Sue's faith would spare the plantation and Nate and her from the ill wind the storm had brought.

Later that year a new man began to visit Mama. Nate felt a little bewildered by his sudden appearance in their lives. He liked to pick up Nate and hold him up in the air, telling him what a cute little boy he was all the while. Nate hated the queasy sensation in his stomach as he rose toward the ceiling and usually shed a few crocodile tears. CW didn't stop doing it though. His goal was to impress Mama with how much he cared for her child, and he succeeded, even before he started to try.

CW was tall, light skinned, high yellow, and handsome. He was different from the other men with whom Mama kept company. CW was looking for a wife, knowing himself well enough to understand he needed a woman to look after him.

One afternoon Nate was playing in a mud puddle in front of the house when he saw Mama come out the front door. She called to him. He was sure that he was going to get a whipping for all the dirt and mud on his little body and clothing. As he approached, he quickly realized he had never seen his Mama look happier or more beautiful.

"Mama," he said, "you are the prettiest lady I ever saw."

Mama smiled and smoothed her hair back on the sides under the white hat she had perched on top of her head. A lavender feather was affixed to the side and a translucent white net fell just over her eyes. Her dress was crisp white cotton, and she wore white stocking and shiny patent leather high heels. Her ensemble had been borrowed from several of her friends and cousins.

"Go on, now, boy. Get cleaned up and put on the pants and shirt I laid out for you. We gotta go soon."

"Where we goin', Mama?"

"Mama's goin' to get married today, child."

After the wedding CW moved into Mama's house and life was good for a couple of months. Nate was happy because his Mama seemed happy for the first time that he could remember. By that time she was six months pregnant with CW's child, and the couple eagerly awaited the birth—together and married. It was everything she had always dreamed about.

The newlyweds wanted more time alone so Nate began to spend weekends with Mom Pearl. Her house was always a flurry of activity—lots of children and grandchildren, Nate's uncles and aunts, not to mention plantation folks stopping by to visit or do business. Mom Pearl was quite an entrepreneur, a real go getter who was always scheming to make extra money. She didn't go into the field much to pick cotton, but her family's quota was met every time because of her many children, seven in all, biological and adopted.

One thing for sure, Mom Pearl was constantly busy. She babysat for most of her many grandchildren. Uncle Joe had ten children, Aunt Lube had six, Aunt Dago had one and Uncle James T had several children with a variety of different women. She also got paid to watch the children of plantation families.

In addition to her babysitting and midwifing, she also made extra cash from her hobby of fishing. She held fish frys most every weekend in the late spring and summer, selling platter of fried fish, potato salad and green salad for one dollar and fifty cents each. The truth was Mom Pearl loved to fish. She enjoyed the peace and quiet. Sometimes she took Nate along, and he also enjoyed the solitude of sitting on the lake bank waiting for the fish to bite almost as much as his grandmother did. In the spring when the trees were blooming and the grass sprouting tender and chartreuse green, Nate relished watching Mom Pearl fish. She threw in the line and hook she had hung on a twelve-foot piece of cane, and the two waited without speaking for a tug on the line. Nate bubbled with excitement as she pulled the fish in and plopped it into the aluminum bucket to take back home. Mom Pearl needed the peace fishing brought her. It was a sharp contrast to the rest of her daily life filled with so many people and so much noise and activity.

Nate was a subdued boy by nature, so resting quietly while Mom Pearl fished was very much in keeping with his character. He watched her intently. Sometimes she dozed, but never so deeply that a pull on her line wouldn't wake her. She was ever vigilant of the task at hand. She pulled in the line and grabbed up the fish. "Lord, look, child, it's a big fat one."

He watched as she removed the hook from its mouth. As was her habit, she held up the shiny, wet fish and surveyed it carefully. If it was too small, she'd throw it back, but this one was nice and big. "Here you go, boy," she said, handing the squirming creature to her grandson.

Nate took hold of the slippery fish, tightly but not too tightly, lest it slip out of his hands. Ever so cautiously, he carried the fish to the bucket and dropped it in with a splash. Mom Pearl watched over his shoulder and praised him for a job well done. He looked back at her and saw the pride in her eyes, and he felt very important.

Mom Pearl was not a handsome woman by any means. Her skin was freckled and appeared discolored in spots. Her teeth were bad with several missing or broken. She constantly dipped snuff and the juice stained the front of all her dresses. But to her grandson Mom Pearl was beautiful.

As they walked back to her house after a successful morning of fishing, she sang church hymns and encouraged Nate to sing along. She had been the first to recognize his outstanding singing voice. She told him, "Boy, keep singing because you've got a beautiful voice."

The house was abuzz with activity. She cleaned the fish and

gave some to her children to take home and feed their families. She fixed up a couple for lunch and fed Nate and whoever else wanted to eat. She was an excellent cook, and Nate, who never got enough to eat at home, ate till his belly nearly burst. Mom Pearl fixed the catfish, brims, white perch and the occasional bass in a mixture of seasoned cornmeal. There was always a big bowl of potato salad and a bowl of mixed greens from her garden. The smells of her kitchen were intoxicating. Mama, always too tired and too broke, never had the wherewithal to care for Nate as his grandmother did.

After lunch was over and the kitchen all cleaned up, Mom Pearl came outside and sat down on the stoop, watching Nate play with her other grandchildren. She didn't get to see him as much as the others and so wanted him to know that his father's family loved him. It broke her heart that her son had denied his own child. To her there was no doubting Nate's parentage.

"Nate, come over and sit with me," she called.

Nate obediently joined her.

"Boy, you know I'm always sayin' you look just like your Daddy, don't you?"

"Yes, maam." He tried not to look as uncomfortable as he felt whenever she said that. He'd never seen his Daddy, and her saying he looked like someone he'd never seen bothered him.

"Lookie here." She reached into the pocket of her dress and pulled out a photograph. "This is your Daddy. You got the same nose and forehead. Look, child."

At first Nate didn't want to, but he obeyed his grandmother. Here was the stranger who had been so absent yet so influential. Nate couldn't tell anything from the picture. "He don't look like me."

"Why sure he does. Look at him. You're the spittin' image of your Daddy."

"Mom Pearl, I can't even see his eyes. Why's he wearin' sunglasses?"

His grandmother explained his father got in a fight a few years back and lost an eye. Ever since he always wore sunglasses.

Nate looked away. He was curious about his father but also

afraid of him. He couldn't' help but be aware of his mother's fear that his Daddy would come and snatch him just as Manual's daddy had. Sometimes Nate lay awake at night fearing this dark stranger who might at any time come and take him from the person he loved the most. Yet something inside him made him want to know his Daddy. It was all too much for a four year old to make sense of.

Mom Pearl could feel his confusion. "Come up here and sit on my lap." Nate climbed up and she held him tightly. She began to sing a hymn softly in his ear. He stayed there for a long while before running back out to play.

The following week Nate and Mama were at home alone in the early afternoon. Mama had just returned from a morning of cooking and cleaning and milking the cows at the big house. CW had gone reluctantly in the morning to work at Mr. Charlie's sawmill. Mama begged him to get to work on time. He didn't want to go at all. "Mr. Charlie will skin you alive if you don't go to work, baby," she told him.

"All right, woman," he said pulling his body up out of bed, "but I aint workin' in the field later on. I'm just too damn tired."

Mama kissed him and said, "I know, baby, that's all right."

CW started to get dress. "What you lookin' at, boy?' he yelled at Nate, who was standing silently watching in the doorway. Nate ran outside. "I swear that boy is always watchin' me. What the hell is the matter with him?"

He finally got off to work. Mama was relieved and breezed through her chores at Miss Ann's. She was in a good mood and was catching up on a few things at home before going out to pick cotton in the afternoon. Through the front door she spied the iceman's truck heading up the road. She had been waiting for him for days, but seemed to miss him each time he drove his route through the plantation. "Wait," she called and ran to catch him. "Wait," she shouted again. She stepped on to porch and started down the steps. She missed one of the top steps and tumbled down landing hard on her stomach. Nate heard Mama scream and ran to help her. She got up and managed to make her way inside where she lay down on the floor. Nate's eyes filled with tears when he saw bright red blood on Mama's dress.

He ran out the door and across the street to fetch Miss Carrie Hall. He begged her to come with him and help his Mama. Miss Carrie took care of Mama, getting her into bed and putting a cool rag on her forehead.

Mama stayed in bed for several days. Soon, however, she resumed her work on the plantation. Sometimes she felt pain in her belly, but after a couple of days she began to feel the baby moving. She and CW were very relieved to know that the baby was all right.

A few months later Mama went into labor. Because of the fall and the potential for complications, Mom Pearl thought it best to call in Dr. Jack Wilson, who doctored for the sharecroppers on Mr. Charlie's plantation. A baby boy was born, but Mama was still having contractions. Dr. Jack felt a second baby and delivered him. The child was stillborn; his head had been crushed in the fall. He had died instantly. Mama carried the dead baby for three months and had no idea she was pregnant with twins.

The surviving twin was named James. James became the apple of his parents' eyes. They thanked the Lord every day that this precious boy had been spared when his little brother had been taken from them. They set about their life together as a little family. Newlyweds with a new baby—it seemed life could not get better unless they had more children of their own.

Nate shared their joy and was excited to have a new baby brother. He tried to help his Mama care of James, but Mama yelled and pushed him away. She fretted over James' health and safety and feared Nate might accidentally harm the infant upon whom all her attention was focused. Increasingly, it appeared Nate didn't fit into the family. His parents began to blame him for everything that went wrong. He felt more and more unwanted.

Chapter Three

In the months after James' birth, Mama and CW became absorbed by the grind of work on the plantation. They rarely had time or energy for each other. While Nate had often seen his parents appearing joyously in love, those occasions were fewer and fewer. Their affection for each other was drowning in the overwhelming stress of struggling to survive.

Nate saw Mama alone and crying more and more frequently. He had overheard Mama telling her friend Carrie Mae about CW and another woman. To make matters worse over the next few years Mama would miscarry two times. Apparently, the fall had damaged her organs. She feared she was no longer capable of carrying a child. Mama was devastated. If she could give CW another baby, he would stop wanting other women. Her family would once again know the happiness James' birth had brought. Mama cried realizing she could no longer bear a child for CW and blamed herself for his infidelity.

Fighting and arguing increased in the house. More and more Nate became the scapegoat for the family's unhappiness. James, the favored child, was above reproach. With every disagreement, every squabble, every pulling of hair, every broken toy, Nate received the blame and the punishment. He was beaten with a stick or a belt several times a week. Sometimes he was beaten until he had bloody wounds. There was rarely if ever a word of praise, encouragement or love for this lonely, battered boy.

Two things were his salvation during this time in his life. Two things allowed him an escape. One of them offered the safe exploration of his mind and character. The other showed him there was another kind of life possible for him.

He discovered his first safe haven quite by accident when he was just five years old. By this time he had longed to run away from home to escape the abuse he suffered on a daily basis. But he knew that was impossible. They'd find him, and when they did he feared they might beat him so badly he would die. He could talk to no one about the abuse, not Mom Pearl, his aunts and uncles, and certainly not Big Mama. He was convinced no one would believe him. Even if they did believe, no one could help him. He was all he had, and he began to rely on his own resources to survive.

One Sunday afternoon, Nate and James were playing in the yard. The two boys devised a game of running up to a puddle and leaping over it, the contest being who could jump the highest and the longest. After several flights through the air, both were determined to make the next one his best. They lined up on either side of the small brown pool and set themselves. Simultaneously they ran toward the obstacle. Nate launched himself and glided upward. James stumbled on take off and with flailing arms and legs clipped Nate's side. The boys went flying onto the dirt. Nate was startled. His knee and elbow were skinned. James began to cry. "You pushed me," he wailed.

"No, I didn't."

"Yes, you did."

"It was an accident."

"It was not. I'm tellin' Daddy," James shouted and headed for the house.

"James, no, don't. I'll kiss it and make it better like Mama does. Please don't tell Daddy…" But it was too late. James was already at the front door. Nate was terrified. He knew too well what was coming. His back was still sore from a whipping the day before. He ran around the back of the house, desperately searching for escape. Falling down to his knees, he clenched his eyes shut furiously fighting his tears. He needed a clear head. He needed to think, to use his brain. It was his only hope.

He opened his eyes and there it was. He had walked right by it a thousand times and never noticed. The house was set up on two-foot concrete blocks with a crawl space underneath. The space between the house and the ground was plenty wide enough for him to slide into. As he stared at the gap, he heard CW shouting, "Nate, come here you little bastard." Nate slid under the house, pulling his arms and legs in until he was completely hidden.

It was dim and cold, but Nate began to relax. Breathing in the smell of the damp earth, he began to feel safe. Up ahead he could see an opening and he slid toward it. In the middle of the underside of the shack was a small space carved out of the dirt at the bottom of the chimney. It was just large enough for him to sit in. There, in the chimney hole, he had found a safe place.

Outside he heard his parents yelling for him, but he ignored them. He stayed right where he was. All the while he talked to himself. Be strong. Be strong. Be strong. He repeated the words over and over in his mind. When he emerged, he was ready for his beating. He was not in control of what happened to him.

The second saving grace came when he was eight years old. One day Mama sent him to school for the first time. It was raining, and plantation folks sent their children to school when it rained and no one could work in the field. Nate didn't know why Mama had suddenly decided to send him, but he gladly embraced the opportunity. Yet he was fearful. He had rarely left the plantation or the neighboring plantations for any reason. Now he would have to venture well beyond the confines, and he would have to go alone.

The other children were no comfort to him. He was a loner and didn't socialize much with other kids, not even his own cousins. He sat alone in the front seat of the broken down, old school bus, his eyes wide with a mixture of fear and anticipation.

Finally, after more than an hour on the back roads of Washington County, the bus pulled up in front of Chatham Elementary School, a segregated school for Negro children. There was another Chatham Elementary in a newer, better building closer to town, but that was for whites only. The white children got the best of everything the state of Mississippi had to offer. Negro children were taught from out of date, hand-me-down textbooks using precious little in the way of supplies.

Chatham was a small white washed, three room schoolhouse, which housed grades one through six. Teachers taught two grade levels at a time to save on space and expenses. Miss Agnes, the principal, met the children as they exited the bus and made sure they all found their classrooms. Nate was assigned to first grade with Miss Miller. He sheepishly entered Miss Miller's room. She greeted him warmly and graciously, wearing a wide, friendly smile. Her voice was soft and comforting, yet firm and assured. He felt instantly secure with her. Miss Miller announced Nate's name to the rest of his class and sent him to his seat. "This is your desk, Nathaniel. You can keep things inside and use it as long as you're in my class."

"Do I have to give it back?" Nate asked. His classmates giggled.

"Why, yes, you do, but when you go to third grade your teacher Miss Vaughn will give you a desk in her classroom."

"Thank you, Miss Miller," Nate replied. He smiled at his teacher, and she smiled back. Her eyes were kind and gentle. They conveyed a positive regard for him. He knew she would take care of him and treat him well. He was certainly not accustomed to being treated like he mattered.

Miss Miller walked up to the chalkboard and began writing letters. "Now, children, take out your paper and write the letter M ten times on the top lines." Nate looked around and saw the others rustling in their desks and pulling out a piece of paper and a pencil. He looked into his desk and found it empty. When he looked up he saw Miss Miller standing in front of him her hand out stretched with paper and a pencil for him. He took the paper and smiled at her.

She went over to the boy next to him and watched him. The other children were all making marks on their papers with the pencil. Nate suddenly felt afraid. He picked up his pencil. Carefully watching the other children, trying to figure out what to do. He felt like crying. But Miss Miller was right there to help him. She gently took his right hand and showed him how to hold the pencil properly. Then she put his hand onto the paper, pressing the pencil point down. She moved his hand up then down then up then down again, forming a perfect letter M. Nate smiled broadly. He was learning to write.

As he rode back to the plantation at the end of his first day at school, Nate knew instinctively that his future lay there. Not only was it the most loving and comfortable place he had ever known, it also presented a new world of learning and exploration. He wanted to go back again and again. Although it was not good for the cotton crop or his family's quota, he secretly began to pray every night for rain the next day so he would be "forced" to attend school.

Later that day Mama got home early from her chores at Miss Ann's. She burst into the house, went immediately into the sleeping room, and pulled the curtain shut. Nate could hear her muffled sobs. He stood outside the doorway listening. "Mama, what's the matter?"

"Nuthin', child."

"Mama, are you okay?" In spite of the abuse she perpetrated and allowed, he still loved her more than all others, including himself. It was his dearest wish to make her proud of him.

After a few moments Mama replied, "Get James ready. We're goin' over to Mama's house."

"Yes, Mama," Nate answered. His heart sank. That was the last place he wanted to go and probably the last place Mama ought to go.

From the minute they arrived, Big Mama wasted no time embarking on a tirade about Mama's stupidity, her bad choices, her poor taste in men.

"Mama, he's got a whore in Greenville. He hasn't been home for days. What should I do?" Mama suddenly burst out.

"You don't do nuthin'. He'll be back when he's ready. Then the two of you can go on with your good for nuthin' lives."

"But how do I stop him from runnin' around?"

"You don't. He's your husband. You made your bed with him and now you gotta lie in it."

Mama sobbed. She wanted so badly to stop him, to go to Greenville, throw herself at his feet and beg him to come home, but she always listened to Big Mama and did whatever Big Mama told her to do.

As Nate listened to the conversation, he became very angry. He didn't like the way Big Mama treated his mother, yet he didn't dare say a word. Mama looked up and saw her son watching them. "Boy, go run along now. Mama don't want you hearin' this."

Nate didn't respond. He was so deep in his own thoughts. "NATE," Mama shouted, "get the hell out of here."

He was startled and quickly turned for the front door wanting to get out as quickly as possible. He didn't want to make Mama any angrier by dawdling. As he moved his hand struck a little blue dime store vase, knocking it to the floor. It shattered. Nate froze in place.

Big Mama got up and got her willow switch. She came toward him wielding the switch while Mama hurriedly swept up the broken glass. Both women were furious with him.

"Get your ass over here, you little shit," Big Mama commanded, slapping the switch on her hand.

Nate was already crying. "Please, Mama, don't let her do it."

Mama frowned at him in disgust. "You get what you deserve," she told him without an ounce of sympathy.

"Get over here," Big Mama boomed. Nate obeyed, pulling up his shirt and laying across a chair. Big Mama began to hit him on the back with the switch that she had fashioned by braiding three willow branches together. She slapped his skin over and over until his back was bleeding.

When she was done, Big Mama put some lard on his wounds to stop the bleeding. "I swear I don't know what to do with that boy. He's got the devil in him," she exclaimed.

The two women went back to talking, leaving Nate alone and crying in the middle of the room while James played happily in the corner.

That night Nate lay on his side till he fell asleep. It was too painful to lie on the fresh wounds on his back. A few hours later he awoke, gripped with fear and panic. He screamed and cried for a long time before Mama approached him. "Nathaniel, stop it. Be quiet and go back to sleep," she told him.

But Nate could not stop. Mama sat down next to him. She just wanted him to stop so she could get some sleep. She threw her arms around him and held him close. Only then did he begin to calm down. Night after night, the same terror revisited him in his sleep. Sometimes even the neighbors heard his cries. Some of them asked Mama what was wrong with her child. Mama made no response. She began to fear what the plantation gossips were already whispering—that her son Nathaniel was crazy.

Callie McDaniel, Big Mama, was the kind of person no one could make happy. She was a plump woman about five feet tall. She took no guff from anyone and had few friends. She mostly shunned outsiders, especially as she got older. In her later years she was fond of saying, "You always help people and when you need somethin', nobody's around. That's why I don't help people no more." She was a bitter old lady. Mama never quite understood she would never earn her mother's respect, so she tried and tried until the day Big Mama died.

One night a storm arose on the plantation. Though not as bad as the one in 1949, the heavens erupted in an awful tumult. Always the dutiful daughter, Mama gathered up her children and headed to Big Mama's house to comfort her through the storm.

Mama knocked hard on the front door. Nate hoped silently that his grandmother was not at home. His backside was still sore from the last beating she had inflicted upon him. She seemed to enjoy hurting him. He hated going to his grandmother's house. He prayed and prayed she would not answer.

Finally, Big Mama flung open the door. She clutched a pile of white bed sheets to her chest. "What in Jesus' name are you doing bringing those children out in such a storm?"

Mama looked as though her mother had slapped her in the face. "Mama, we came to keep you company. We know how scared you get."

Big Mama frowned at her daughter. "Well, come on inside. You look like a bunch of hobos." She strained to throw a sheet over the last exposed window. "Willie," she shouted, " go get you some rags and wipe those boys' heads before they catch their deaths. What kind of mother are you?"

"Yes, Mama."

Nate gritted his teeth as he listened to Big Mama insult his mother. Mama came up behind him and roughly dried his head.

The old woman groaned as she sat down on her favorite wooden rocker. She picked up her pipe and filled it with three fingers of George Washington tobacco. She lit the bowl with a shaky hand

and puffed. The smoke traveled up the hollow barrel, and the tobacco crackled as it burned.

The windows flashed with a bolt of lightening. The boom that followed shook the house. "Lord almighty, God sure is angry this evenin'," she said. "Come and sit by your grandma," she said to James, who obediently moved and sat by her leg.

Nate was relieved she hadn't asked him to sit closer. She always smelled like a strange mixture of tobacco smoke, coal oil liniment, and Dog Man hair grease. The odor made him nearly sick to his stomach.

"Callie..." a voice called from the bedroom.

Big Mama let out a sigh of disgust. "I swear that man is such a good for nuthin' baby."

"Should I go see what he wants?" Mama asked.

"Don't you move, girl. Just tend your boys." Big Mama put down her pipe and yelled to the back room. "Get your ass out of bed and come out here if you want somethin'"

After awhile Paw Paw stumbled into the room. He was hung over. His eyes were red and swollen. Nate watched him sympathetically. He liked his grandfather. Paw Paw was always nice to him. When he reached the middle of the room. Paw Paw stopped. It took him a few minutes to orient himself. He moved backward then forward and made his way over to his tattered armchair feeling his way with his cane. He sat down.

Big Mama laughed at him. "You are a worthless old man," she said to him, "Worthless."

Paw Paw made no reaction. He was used to the abuse and tolerated it. Another gristle back man, a man with no backbone. It was probably why the marriage had lasted so long. That and the gallons of liquor he drank. Drinking, though, had been one of the few things he and his wife had in common. In the old days they'd go down to the Green Frog juke house and drink all night long. Big Mama's health was never that good, and she finally had to stop drinking because of her high blood pressure. When she drank she had been prone to alcoholic seizures. Nate had seen her many a time foaming at the mouth and shaking. Each time he had thought she was going to die. Each time he thought, if she dies now she won't be able to whip me ever again. Each time he'd feel guilty for what he had thought.

While Big Mama and her daughter went to gather blankets for the boys, Nate went over and sat on the arm of Paw Paw's chair. Paw Paw had an odd smile on his face; his eyes were nearly closed. He pulled a hand rolled cigarette from his pocket. As he lit the end the match flame rose inches above the skinny white paper roll. He stopped and told Nate, "Don't you be like me, boy."

He puffed at his cigarette and was silent for a while. He blew a few smoke rings and Nate smiled watching them slowly spread wider and then disappear.

"Hmmmm, boy, you know, one day I'm gonna leave the plantation," Paw Paw mused.

"Where you gonna go, Paw Paw?"

Paw Paw rubbed his chin. "Hmmmm, I don't know, boy. I don't know."

As he watched the last of Paw Paw's smoke rings float to the ceiling, Nate knew deep down he had the same dream as grandfather.

Although no one could have known it, a seed was about to be planted that would slowly blossom into Nate's way off the plantation. Mr. Sylvester lived on Mr. Tater William's plantation. He was a religious man married to Miss Everline with a family of six children, Sam, Les, Lil' Buddy, Dorothy, Preston, and Joanne. His son Les was born with a growth on his backbone. The doctor made a hole in the growth, apparently to drain it, but through some error in placement or judgment, Les was left permanently paralyzed following the procedure. Mr. Sylvester and Miss Everline worked hard to support their family and care for their handicapped child. With no wheel chair or special equipment of any kind, Les had to be carried wherever he went.

The hardships of his life only deepened Mr. Sylvester's faith, and he was a prominent member of his plantation's Baptist church. He was a kind man who wanted to share his faith in God with others so that they would know the comfort he felt.

He met young Nate when Nate was picking up pecans on Mr. Tater's plantation to make extra money for his family. He had known of Nate and Mama long before in the small world of the sharecroppers. As he watched Nate make quick work of a patch of ripe cotton plants, he was impressed by Nate's skill and determination. At the end of the day he approached the boy and asked him if he'd like to come to church with his family on Sunday. Nate eagerly told him he would like to go.

Mr. Sylvester would pick up Nate the following Sunday. Nate had agonized over what to wear. His clothes were old and worn. There was nothing fine enough to wear to church. On Saturday he washed out a pair of khaki pants and a faded plaid shirt, but in the crisp, cool light of Sunday morning, the ensemble seemed too common and plain to wear to God's house.

Nate was very excited to be going to church. He had gone a few times with Mama when she had the energy to finish her chores at Miss Ann's and get the family rounded up and off to worship. In his mind, Nate imagined what he should wear. He saw himself proudly marching down the aisle between the wooden benches decked out in a beautiful brown suit with a brown striped tie on a white dress shirt. On his feet he'd wear a shiny pair of brown leather wing tip shoes. That's what he should wear to enter God's house.

His attention returned to the paltry clothing he owned. For a moment, he almost decided not to go, so ashamed he was, but he soon resigned himself to wear the only decent outfit he had. He was thankful at least that no one would see his underwear, which was filled with holes and littered with stains.

When Mr. Sylvester came by to get him, Nate was ready to go. Mr. Sylvester was happy and cheerful, telling Nate about the good news he would hear at church. Nate listened and smiled. Few of the men he had met on the plantation seemed as joyous as Mr. Sylvester or as kind.

The church was full that Sunday. The family could barely find a place to sit together. Soon the preacher stepped up to the podium. Nate listened intently as he talked about forgiveness. He told his flock that to forgive was the way to Jesus and the way to eternal happiness. His words made Nate sad. He realized there were people in his life he could never forgive. The hatred he felt for Big Mama and Mr. Charlie was too strong. He feared he would never know the happiness that the preacher spoke of with such fervent tones.

Miss Everline sat next to him. She fanned herself with a yellowed paper fan with a picture of an angel printed on the topside. She had her eyes closed tight and a smile on her face. Suddenly she cried out hallelujah and jumped up to her feet, her arms raised up in the air. Nate was startled. As suddenly as she jumped up she sat back down and continued to fan her face and neck. She never opened up her eyes.

The preacher stepped away from his podium and a group of men and women stood up on the right side of the front of the church. A gray haired lady in a baby blue dress sat down at the spinet piano and began to play. The group of men and women began to sing, loudly and joyously, singing of the Lord. They clapped their hands and moved their bodies from side to side in unison. Nate was enthralled. Sheepishly at first he began to clap along with them. Miss Everline saw him struggling. "Go on, boy, clap those hands," she told him. "Let the Lord know you love him." Nate began to clap his hands to the beat like he meant it. He felt good. Very good.

The choir invited the congregation to sing along. Miss Everline showed Nate the words to the song printed in an old tattered hymnal. Although he couldn't read most of the words, he listened to those around him and mimicked their words. Nate sang from the depths of his heart. He could scarcely remember feeling so happy in all his life.

Miss Louis Pratt and Miss Minnie Barksdale, two elder spinsters, heard Nate singing. After the service, they pulled Mr. Sylvester aside and told him Nate had a born talent for singing. They wondered if Nate would like to sing for the church next Sunday. "Come here, Nathaniel," Mr. Sylvester called to Nate who was sitting on the steps of the church by himself. Nate came over and Mr. Sylvester asked him if he'd like to sing at church. Nate smiled broadly and told him he would. Miss Pratt went back in the church and gave him a hymnal. She flipped through the pages and found a song for him. She sang the song from start to finish so Nate could learn the melody. "You just learn the words. I'll take care of the rest."

Fortunately that week there were two days of rain. Nate asked

Miss Miller to help him read the words of the hymn. She graciously agreed. She pulled a desk chair next to his and began to help him sound out the letters. Nate struggled, but in a few days, he had memorized the words to the song. He practiced singing it over and over so much so his family got tired of it. "Nathaniel, you aint singin' that God damned song again. Get on outside before I whip your butt raw," Big Mama yelled. Even James spoke up. "Yeah, get out of here. You drivin' me crazy." After that Nate did his rehearsing outside, in the cotton field, sitting among the rows of ripe plants. Soon he was singing the song as he worked, and the folks on the plantation were amazed by his wonderful voice.

Word got around that young Nate was to sing at church on Sunday. The turn out was big. Many of the sharecroppers from Nate's plantation came just to hear their boy sing. No one from Nate's family came.

When the time came for Nate to sing, he walked up to the front of the church without fear. The pianist began the introduction, and Nate closed his eyes just like Miss Everline did when she sang. The music poured out of him, and as he sang and the notes escaped his throat he felt his chest fill up with a sweet and happy feeling as though his heart was being healed. Before he knew it, the song was over. He opened his eyes to see Miss Pratt wiping a tear from her eye with a lavender handkerchief.

Everyone was talking about Nate's voice, how beautiful and expressive it was. As they walked to the plantation store, Miss Pratt told Mama that Nate's singing made her cry it was so beautiful. Mama thanked her and quickly walked away. "Now that boy's gonna think he's too good for us. Already thinkin' he need to go to school. That child is getting too big for his britches, that's for sure," she thought to herself.

Chapter Four

Sun Hall lived in the house across the road from Mama's. He was an entrepreneur of sorts who ran a small juke house on the plantation financed by the meager funds he made as Mr. Charlie's head truck driver. It was steady work hauling logs from the woods to Mr. Charlie's sawmill. Sun was a tall, strong man and a hard worker, very valuable to Mr. Charlie's business, and he was well paid by plantation standards.

Sun had a mean streak and a quick temper. He always carried a gun. Although he had trappings of a normal family life—married to the lovely, light skinned Miss Carrie—he had a dark side. A few years back, as was common knowledge, Sun Hall had killed a man named Nettie.

That day Sun and Nettie had been at Sun's house all afternoon drinking corn whiskey. They laughed and told stories, and after a while both were quite intoxicated. Miss Carrie hovered around them until Sun became annoyed with her. "Get out. Go see your sister. We don't want you 'round here buggin' us, woman," Sun shouted at his wife.

Miss Carrie knew to obey or she'd get a smack across the mouth, so she immediately walked out the door without a word. As she made her way to her sister's house, tears welled in her eyes. She had an awful feeling in the pit of her stomach. Something bad was going to happen, but she could do nothing to stop it.

After Miss Carrie left, Sun's mood blackened. His mind started to race. Nettie's voice grated on his nerves. He watched the man take a long drink of his whiskey. Sun realized he never liked Nettie much. "Why don't you go on, get out of here," Sun told Nettie.

"Man, what you talkin' 'bout? I aint finished my drink."

Sun stroked his Hitler moustache and saw Nettie chuckle in disbelief of his buddy's request. Sun stood up, stumbling to one side before he righted himself. "I said get out of my house."

Now Nettie was annoyed. "Nah, I aint goin' nowhere."

Sun's eyes narrowed. "Get out of my house or I'll shoot you."

"You asshole," Nettie yelled, slurring his words, "shut up and pour me some more whiskey."

A grin spread over Sun's face. It was a cold, dark smile. He pulled out his gun and shot Nettie dead.

Sun was arrested and convicted of Nettie's murder. He spent a few months in jail for the crime, but Mr. Charlie soon got him released. Mr. Charlie needed him back on the plantation. Not having the strong back of Sun Hall was an economic hardship that Mr. Charlie's white friends in the courthouse could relate to. The fact that he had murdered another black man was irrelevant.

But folks on the plantation were justly afraid of Sun Hall. They flinched when he walked too close and generally tried to steer clear of him. And Sun Hall liked it that way.

Miss Miller's voice was sweet and soothing. She sounded like an angel. Each afternoon following lunch and recess, she instructed the class to lay their heads down on the arms of their desks while she read them a story. Nate loved to listen to the fascinating worlds of the stories she told in her soft tones.

The story that day was about a beautiful princess who lived alone in a tall tower. With the side of his cheek pressed against the smooth varnished desk, he popped open his eyes. Most of the children had drifted off to sleep. Nate wanted to stay awake. Whenever he had fallen asleep during naptime at school, he awoke to the feeling that the classroom had turned around. The momentary disorientation scared him so much that he vowed not to fall asleep at school again.

But he felt very tired. The evening before he had experienced a night terror again and had lay awake most of the night. Only the joyous sound of driving rain on the roof of the shack and the promise of a day at school could have roused him that morning.

He felt his eyes falling shut. No, he thought. He tried to raise his head from the desk.

"Come on, Nathaniel, lay your head down and rest," whispered Miss Miller into his ear. He breathed in her scent of lavender water and relaxed. "It's okay. You'll be just fine," she told him. "I'm right here to keep you safe."

His eyes closed and he fell asleep. When he awoke he saw Miss Miller's soft brown eyes watching him and he was all right. He sat up and stretched his arms over his head. The nap lasted only a half hour or so, but it was the most peaceful sleep he could remember. He soon began to look forward to naptime as much as learning at school.

But if the truth were known he most looked forward to the hours he spent with Miss Miller. She was so kind, like a mother to him. But she treated him better than his own Mama. He loved Miss Miller. His heart rose when he saw her. He beamed with pride nearly to bursting when she praised his work. He felt no harm could come to him when he was with her. Yet felt guilty. She was not his mother, and he never wanted Mama to find out how he felt about his teacher. He would die before he would betray Mama.

School was not entirely a pleasant place for Nate in spite of all its goodness. When the children went on the schoolyard at lunch, he always hung around the back of the school while the others ate the chunks of cheese, bread, chicken meat and ripe red apples they brought in their brown paper sacks. Nate never brought his lunch. There was no food at Mama's to take to school, so he went hungry. He surely did not want the children to know he had no food to eat. So he hid from them every school day.

He rested his back against the white washed sidewall of the school and waited. He gazed up at the sky. It was filled with billowy clouds that had brought the rain that morning and threatened to bring more, but the rain had stopped. He shut his eyes and began to think about his future life. Deep in his heart he knew he wanted more than Mama and CW. He dreamed that his life would be different, that he would leave the plantation and he was just beginning to learn how to make that so.

After awhile he figured the children were finished eating, so he headed back to the yard. He stood off to the side watching the children run and laugh and play. A boy named Joshua approached him. Nate tried to look away, but Joshua was staring right into his eyes. Finally, Nate had no choice but to look at him.

Joshua chewed on a piece of straw grass as he surveyed him squinting as the yellow sun emerged from behind the clouds. "My Daddy drives a big tractor."

"So..." Nate replied. A couple of kids noticing the scene came up and stood behind Joshua, watching.

"What does your Daddy do?" Joshua asked Nate.

"He aint got no Daddy," taunted a tall skinny boy from over Joshua's shoulder.

"I do have a Daddy," Nate said loudly, but he only half believed his words. He felt angry and humiliated.

"No you don't," Joshua retorted.

"Yes I do." He tried to be firm but his voice cracked with emotion. The muscles in his temples tightened. He was determined not to cry.

"No, you don't."

"Yes, I do."

Joshua got a big grin on his face, exposing his too large white buckteeth. "Well, let's see him then."

Nate continued to stare into Joshua's face. His eyes burned with pure hatred for him, while inside he screamed. He hadn't even ever seen his father. "Leave me alone," he yelled at the boy.

Joshua stepped back. The game was over. He turned to the other boys. "See, I told ya." They all laughed, and Nate just stood there not knowing what to do. Defeated. The boys' attention on him was short lived, and they ran off still to play kick ball, still laughing at him.

Nate began to feel light headed. He looked toward the school house. The white edges seemed to blend into the white and blue of the sky. He recognized the hazy form of his teacher coming toward him. "Nathaniel, are you all right?"

"No, ma'am. I don't feel so good."

"Well, come on then. Let's get you a drink." She put her arm around his shoulders and walked him to the pipe and spigot in front of the school where the children came to fill the cups they had brought with them from home. "Where's your cup, child?"

Nate stared at the grass. "Where's your cup?"

"I don't have one, ma'am. My Mama don't' have none to give me."

Miss Miller's brow furrowed as she gazed at him. "Come with me. I got a trick to teach you." She took him inside and sat him down in front of the window. She pulled a thick sheet of paper from her desk and showed him how to make a cup good enough for a couple of drinks.

They went back outside to the spigot and filled the fragile cup to the brim. He eagerly drank the lukewarm water and felt so much better. "Thank you, Miss Miller,' he said. He wanted to remain polite and reserved. He didn't want to show the love that he felt for her, but a big smile spread across his face and he looked right into her sweet brown eyes.

"I'm sure you are more than welcome, young man." She smiled back and reached over and gave him a hug. Nate held on and wished that moment would never end.

"Now, come on, let's get back to work," Miss Miller said and she turned and called the children back inside.

As Nate walked back to class he caressed the little cup in his hands. It was the most wonderful thing anyone had ever given him. From that day on he was able to quench his thirst at school instead of going all day without a drink. But more importantly a bellyful of water made it easier to ignore the pangs of hunger that constantly tormented him.

The next day was Saturday. It was the first sunny morning after three days of rain and three blessed days at school for Nate. Mama had left for work that morning leaving Nate in charge of James. Nate had been James' babysitter as long as he could remember. It was hard work. James was a spoiled child. He refused to listen to Nate and knew there would be no consequences for his disobedience when Nate was in charge.

The day was hot and humid. Too warm to stay inside. So the boys went out in the yard. Nate tossed a ragged baseball in the air, always with an eye on his little brother. He took his job seriously. Of course, James did not take Nate seriously. James grew bored with the rusty toy truck he was ramming into a mound of dirt. He stood up and spied a much more interesting prize—Otis' old Chrysler sitting in the front yard. The tires were gone and it sat on rims. The windshield was cracked, the seats ripped, and the side panels dented, but to James it looked as good as Mr. Charlie's shiny new, baby blue Impala. He squealed, jumped in the air and made a beeline for the old wreck.

Nate ran in front of him. "No, you don't," he said sternly. "Mama don't want us goin' around Teenie's car."

James pushed by him. He jiggled the door handle and got inside. Nate grabbed his forehead in frustration. James would not obey him no matter what. There was no bond between the brothers at all. Still Nate begged him to come out of the car, knowing that if anything happened to James... He didn't even want to think about it.

"James, come out, please." But James was having far too much fun. He sat in the driver's seat, moving the steering wheel from side to side, loudly imitating the vroom of a zooming engine. Boldly he reached out and blared the horn.

"James, come on, people's gonna hear ya," Nate said. He looked around expecting Mama to come running up and grab him by the nape of the neck. But all the adults were hard at work and no one came to investigate.

Before Nate knew it, James had crawled into the back seat. He sat on the passenger side banging the back of his little head against the vinyl seat back. Nate tried again and again to get him to come out. He had a sick feeling in his stomach like something real bad was going to happen. He kept checking behind him, hoping Mama wasn't coming toward him with a switch. "James," he yelled again. But it was no use.

As James crawled back over the front seat, a lone wasp stung him just under the eye. He screamed. Nate came running. As James wailed, Nate pulled out the stinger. He took him into the house and put a cool, wet rag over his eye. It was already beginning to swell.

When Mama came home she was furious with Nate. James, who had calmed down, started to wail again as soon as he saw her. Nate tried to explain what had happened. He warned James to get out of the car, but he wouldn't listen. He had yelled and yelled for him to come out, but he wouldn't listen. "Get the hell away from me and my baby," Mama screamed. "You are no good for nuthin'"

Late that evening Teenie stumbled through the screen door. He came by to visit with Mama. When he saw James and heard what had happened, he went after Nate. He grabbed Nate's arm and pulled him into the sleeping room. Nate knew better than to try to defend himself. It would only make things worse. Teenie threw him on the floor, placed his right foot on the side of his neck to hold him down, and began to beat his backside with a machine belt. Nate cried out in pain. He fought the tears, but soon they flowed, hot and stinging. Teenie kept beating him until he stopped hollering. Then he threw down the belt and left the room. Nate lay on the floor whimpering.

After awhile Nate went out the door and crawled under the house and sat in the cold of the chimney hole for a very long time. He reckoned this was about the worst day of his life so far. He comforted himself by dreaming of leaving the plantation one day. Paw Paw said it without even knowing what it meant or having any idea how to do it. Nate would leave the plantation. Nate knew deep in his heart he would make a better life for himself and his Mama.

Chapter Five

Miss Pat banged on Mama's door early one morning. "Willie B, Willie B," she called in a crackly voice.

Mama left her sewing and came to the door. "Morning, Miss Pat. How are you today?"

Miss Pat ignored Mama's greeting. "Just thought you'd wanna know, Dr. Jack's here."

Mama got defensive. "Why would I wanna know?"

"You better take your boy to see him, Willie B."

"I don't need to…"

"Yes, you do. You best see what the doctor says."

Mama was too embarrassed to respond. She knew exactly what Miss Pat meant. The doctor could tell her if her son Nathaniel was crazy. Her eyes welled up with tears.

Miss Pat felt sorry for Mama. "Come on now, child. You gotta take him," she told Mama. " Dr. Jack might be able to fix him right up. You never know unless you find out."

"I guess you're right," Mama said.

"Why sure I am. Now you take him on over, you hear?"

"I will, Miss Pat." Mama knew she had to do something. Just the other morning after Nate was up screaming and crying half the night, Sun Hall approached her as she was walking to the fields. "I heard that damn bastard boy of yours wailing all night. Woke me up out of a dead sleep," he said. His hair was all nappy and sticking out on the sides. His eyes were blood shot and red.

Mama knew it was not good to get Sun Hall angry. "I'm real sorry, Sun."

"I swear that child is crazy. What is wrong with him?" he said as he stormed off in another direction.

After Miss Pat had gone, Mama sat on the stoop wondering if Sun had been right, if the gossip on the plantation was right.

She marched Nate down to Mr. Charlie's office where Dr. Jack set up his makeshift examining room. Every few months he spent an afternoon there doctoring plantation folk. Most of his patients were pregnant women and babies. The adults generally saw him only as a last resort. It was just too expensive. For the most part they relied on home remedies—plant poultices, homemade elixirs, field herbs and plants, and dime store salves.

After waiting an hour or so, Dr. Jack called Willie B inside. Mama sat Nate on the wooden chair that served as the examining table. Dr. Jack was a tall, lanky gray haired man with a handlebar moustache and silver wire framed spectacles with thick coke bottle lenses. "What seems to be the problem?" he asked looking at Willie over the top of his glasses.

Mama launched into a rambling explanation of her son's odd behavior as the doctor listened intently. When she finished he walked across the room without saying a word. Then he doubled back and stopped in front of Mama. "I'm afraid your boy is mentally incompetent."

Mama's mouth dropped open from the shock of his words. She realized Nate was different, but she never imagined it was so serious. "Can't you do somethin' for him?"

"There's nothing I can do. I'm so sorry."

Mama's hand went up and covered her mouth. She felt like she had been stuck in the stomach. "Nuthin' at all?"

"No. He'll probably need to be watched and taken care of the rest of his life."

The room was quiet. Nate stared at the doctor, who had made no effort to conceal his diagnosis from him. He didn't understand why Dr. Jack had said such awful things about him. He only knew his Mama was really upset. He went over to her and tried to comfort her, but she shrugged him off. "Don't worry, Mama. It's not true. I know it's not true. You'll see."

Mama started to cry. Oh my God, she thought. He's so crazy he doesn't even know he's crazy. She quickly collected herself. "Thank you, doctor," she said and hurried out of the room with her son.

News that Dr. Jack had said Nate was crazy spread across the plantation like wildfire. Everyone was whispering about Willie B's crazy child. Even Mr. Charlie was privy to the news. He wasn't in the least surprised. He already suspected as much. Mama was so ashamed that she avoided speaking to anyone except her family for weeks.

One evening Mama came home long after sundown. Nate gave her some flour bread with flour gravy he had made. He put some of the apples Mama had canned on the plate. She ate up the meager food. She talked softly about the gossip she'd heard in the field that day, failing to notice that Nate had swept the house and wiped down the table and chairs. When she finished the eating, Nate walked her to her bed. He got some water and asked her to hang her feet over the side. He took a rag made of one of James' baby shirts and dipped it into the cool water, rubbed it on a bar of soap and gently washed her tired calloused feet. When he finished, he looked up to see her fast asleep. He lifted her feet onto the stir mattress. The old springs creaked and he feared she might wake, but her snoring continued. Her eyes stayed closed. As he pulled up the tattered quilt that Big Mama had given them, he wondered what would have become of her if not for him.

So weak and simple she was—unable to read or even write her own name. She missed her childhood and the chance to go to school. She was ignorant. She couldn't keep the money the family made. She was completely incapable of imagining a life outside the plantation. Unaccustomed to freedom, completely bound to Mr. Charlie, overflowing with fear and uncertainty, she attached herself to the men of the plantation. Nate watched and gritted his teeth as loser after loser trotted in and out of her life. Her current husband CW was certainly no prize, but at least he had done her the honor of marrying her. Sometimes he wanted to scream at her, "What are you doing with him? Why do you let him treat you that way?" But he could never actually criticize her. It was his job to care for her and make her life as bearable as possible. Mama was a lost soul and he was the only one on whom she could depend—whether she knew it or not.

Nate lay down on the bed next to her. The shack was cold that night. Pulling the threadbare quilt up around his neck, he shivered. He prayed he would sleep through the night, that his night terrors would not visit him for one evening.

The front screen door slammed. CW stumbled in, drunk again. Nate heard him rustling through the bedroom, the clank of his belt buckle against the iron of the bed frame. He moaned as he lay down. His back was aching. Even the corn whiskey hadn't taken the pain away. James shouted something incoherent in his sleep. CW laughed at his son, "What's the matter, boy?" But James didn't stir.

Nate drifted to sleep, but awoke with a start, overcome, wailing, crying, inconsolable. There was fear and panic in his stomach. He felt of creeping fingers of terror wrapping around his heart, stealing his breath. He gasped for air. "Nate, stop it now," Mama moaned. "Damn you, crazy boy, stop it."

"That boy oughta be locked up somewhere," CW said.

Mama and CW ignored him as best they could and fell back to sleep. After an hour or so, Nate mercifully did the same.

Nate awoke just as the sun was rising. His muscles ached from a long day of picking cotton the day before. His haul was 350 pounds. He was relieved knowing it would ease the burden on the family. The sun peeked over the horizon. The sky was bright, deep blue with only a wisp of a cloud skirting across. Nate groaned with disappointment. There would be no school that day. He glanced at the worn pair of khaki pants and the hand me down plaid shirt he'd washed out and carefully hung to dry. He'd be wearing his field overalls today.

He threw some cold water on his face from the aluminum basin and pulled on his clothes. As he tied his tattered shoes, he noticed the sole was pulling away again where he had glued it only a week ago. He prayed that this year they'd get a settlement bonus at the end of harvest season so maybe he could get a new pair.

The rest of the family began to awaken. CW moaned with pain. His back locked up. He could barely move. He walked out of the sleeping room hunched over at the waist, unable to straighten up. Mama gently rubbed his back. "Stop it. Stop it," he snapped. "It don't make it no better."

"But I..." Mama stammered.

"It don't do no good."

"How are you gonna make it to the mill today?"

"I just can't."

"Oh, I don't know. Mr. Charlie, he'll be fit to..."

"Shut up woman. What else can I do?" CW shouted at her.

As Mama walked away wrapping a rag around her head, Nate caught her eyes. She quickly looked away, but he saw the tears. She was terrified of what would happen when Mr. Charlie realized her husband was not at work.

"James, get dressed," Mama called. Completely unaware, James sat in the corner playing with some sticks and a couple pinecones. He didn't move.

Nate heard Mama and CW whispering. He went over to the doorway to see what they were doing. Mama lifted the cover of the stir mattress and helped CW crawl inside. She patted the cotton boles around him so his body was hidden and then she pulled the canvas cover over him. She turned and looked directly at Nate. "You stay quiet, you hear? If Mr. Charlie comes don't you tell him where CW is. Don't say a word now."

"I won't, Mama. I'll be quiet."

"And you boys be ready when I get back from the big house." She fixed her gingham apron around her waist and headed out the door to milk Miss Ann's cows and fix Miss Ann's breakfast.

The house was quiet except for the thudding of the red rubber ball James bounced against the wall. Nate stood in the middle of the eating room. He was scared. He had heard the men talking down at the plantation store. A young black man at Mr. Cooper's plantation wasn't pulling his weight in the fields and one day he had cursed at the boss man. He disappeared that night and in the morning they found him laying in a pig trough, his arm broken and his face bloody. "He was damn lucky to be alive," Jimmy Lee had told the other men.

Nate waited anxiously for Mama to return. He scrubbed the floor with lye water and a wooden brush. The minutes passed slowly. James laughed and jumped in the wet spots. Nate yelled at him to stop, but James kept hopping from spot to spot, giggling all the while.

The screen door suddenly creaked open. Nate was relieved thinking it was Mama, but when he looked up he saw the flash of Mr. Charlie's eye glasses. His face was bright red; veins bulged in his long skinny neck. Two other white men were with him. "Where the hell is he?" one of the men asked Nate.

Nate was too scared to speak.

"Answer me boy."

"Don't bother with him," Mr. Charlie told his cohort. "He's crazy as a loon."

Nate stared at the men. His eyes wide with fear.

"Start searchin' and don't stop till you find that sorry-assed nigger."

The white men threw over benches and knocked things around. Nate clenched his eyes shut and backed into the corner. James ran over to him, crying. Nate grabbed hold of his brother and squeezed him tightly. Please don't find him. Please don't find him. He prayed over and over.

Mr. Charlie spied movement in the stir mattress and when the men threw it over, CW tumbled out. "Get up," said Mr. Charlie. He kicked CW square in the back.

CW howled in pain. "Mr. Charlie, sir, my back's hurtin' so bad I can hardly move."

"Get your ass up and get out to the car, nigger." He continued to kick CW as he nearly crawled outside. Nate watched from the doorway. CW was not even permitted to put clothes on over his skivvies. Mr. Charlie became impatient and picked up CW by the elastic band of his under shorts and threw him into the back of the car. CW screamed.

Nate stood in the doorway and watched. His heart burned with hatred for that evil man. He swore one day he would kill Mr. Charlie.

When CW returned that evening he was battered and still bleeding. Mama washed his wounds with hot rags. There was no thought of skipping work tomorrow.

Chapter Six

The plantation store was a wonderland of smells and tastes and colors. For a boy who was always going hungry, sometimes just walking through the store, taking a long deep breath and gazing at the wrapped up chunks and morsels provided enough strength to make it through an afternoon with no lunch or an evening without supper.

Mr. Charlie ran the store and was fond of working there. He hired a clerk here and there, but he usually ended up firing them. No one could do the job as well as he could. He was a hard man to please.

He didn't much like when children came into the store and loitered around without buying anything. Daily he angrily chased out the little malingerers. Nate, however, felt it was surely worth incurring Mr. Charlie's wrath for a few minutes of heaven. He learned to sneak in behind white folks who came in to do some shopping. While Mr. Charlie was showing them to the St. Joseph's aspirin or the Calumet baking powder, nearly tripping over himself to be uncharacteristically courteous, Nate had the perfect opportunity to savor the store's sights and smells.

Usually he started with the meat counter, lingering over the long rolls of hog head sass, salami and bologna. His favorite was the hog head sass, pickled meat with flecks of green and red pepper and spices. Two slices fit on a stage plank, a rectangular honey graham cookie with purple icing that came two to a pack. The resulting sandwich was delectable, enough to satisfy a young boy's empty belly. A long necked bottle of ice-cold Barques root beer was just the thing to wash it down. Nate could taste the sweetness of the icing against his tongue and feel the root beer foaming around his mouth as he chewed. The whole treat, root beer and all, would have cost him only twenty-five cents, but it was a quarter he would save today. His fantasy lunch would have to do.

He moved on to the candy counter as Mr. Charlie guffawed in the background at something the white folks had said. Here was the greatest temptation of all. His mind began to spin as he surveyed the red and white peppermints, blue and orange jawbreakers, bright yellow Butterfingers, and his favorite—red, white and blue Baby Ruth bars.

A few months back the irresistible Baby Ruths had gotten him into trouble. Nate had gone to the store that day with a boy named Jesse Henry. Jesse had some money, fifty cents or so, and was going to buy something to eat. Nate didn't have any money, so Jesse agreed to distract old Ed, Mr. Charlie's clerk, so Nate could take something.

"Gimme a hunk a salami," Jesse said to the clerk. As Ed went behind the counter to cut the salami, Nate approached the register. He sneaked behind the counter and grabbed a whole, precious box of Baby Ruths and slipped out the door.

Jess watched him go and choked back a snicker. "Gimme a stage plank to go with it," he said as Ed returned with the salami.

Ed raised his head and looked around the store. "Hey, where'd that other boy go?"

"I dunno," Jesse said innocently.

Later that day Ed noticed the box of Baby Ruths was missing. He told Mr. Charlie he thought the boy with Jesse had taken it. He couldn't be sure, but he thought that boy was Nate. Mr. Charlie was furious, but he quickly realized Nate was Willie B's crazy son. His anger was a bit muted. No use getting upset over a nigger with a few screws loose. He figured he'd just have to try and make the best of it. He marched over to Mama house and confronted her.

"Couldn't have been my boy. He been with me all day." But Mama was scared. After Mr. Charlie left, Nate offered to pay for the Baby Ruths just to make Mama feel better. Once he got his money, Mr. Charlie was satisfied and never brought up the matter again.

As he remembered the trouble the irresistible candies had caused, Nate stared longingly at the forbidden Baby Ruth bars.

"Oh, what an adorable little colored boy," exclaimed the white woman as she piled her purchases next to the register.

Nate looked up and smiled at her sheepishly. He stepped back from the candy counter. He'd hoped to sneak out before Mr. Charlie finished with the white folks, but it was too late. Mr. Charlie's face reddened when he saw Nate. He raised a pale, bony finger and pointed to the door. "Get the hell out of my store, boy."

Nate ran out the door, almost bumping into the white lady's husband. "Damn crazy child," muttered Mr. Charlie and then he turned and smiled almost sweetly at his customers.

Christmastime was approaching. Miss Miller had the classroom decorated with cardboard Santas and reindeer. Nate thought it looked beautiful. At lunchtime Miss Miller asked Nate to stay behind. The other children dashed to the playground, leaving Nate and Miss Miller alone. Nate wondered if he had done something wrong. He remembered Joshua getting called to stay at lunch, and when the kids returned he was standing in the corner. Nate waited nervously at his desk.

"Come up here, Nathaniel. I have something for you," Miss Miller said.

Nate got up and walked up to her desk. She was wearing a powder blue dress with white flowers. Her hair was done up in a bun on top of her head and golden earrings dangled from her ear lobes.

She reached into the top drawer of her desk and took out a package wrapped in red paper with angels printed on it. Atop the package was a crisp red bow. "I'm going to give the others their gifts later, but I wanted to give this to you special."

Nate hesitated. No one had given him a gift before. He didn't know what to do.

"Go on. Open it."

He gingerly took the box and looked at it for a few seconds. He looked up at Miss Miller.

"Go on, child. It's for you."

He began to rip the wrapping paper, but suddenly stopped. He had forgotten to thank her. "Thank you, Miss Miller."

"You are truly welcome, young man. Now open it. I can't stand the suspense."

Nate smiled at her and tore off the rest of the paper, revealing a small brown box. He took off the lid and there was a red rubber ball, a pencil sharpener, and a red plastic telescoping drinking cup. He pulled the cup open and marveled at it.

"Now you have your own cup. No more paper ones," Miss Miller said sweetly.

"Yes, ma'am." He was so overcome he didn't know what else to say. He just stared and stared at the gift she had given him.

"Why don't you go out and fill it with water and have a drink with the rest of the children?"

"Yes, ma'am." He moved to run outside and then turned around. "Thank you very much, Miss Miller."

Nate would keep the precious gifts from his teacher well into his adulthood as most treasured possessions.

Christmastime was also settlement time. Nate was sure this year for the first time his family would get a bonus. He had worked so hard making the family's quota and then some.

Often he worked into the night when the moonshine provided enough light for picking. Nate had a talent for picking cotton and made good use of it every chance he got. He picked more cotton than the rest of his family combined. Surely, the family would be rewarded this year.

He dreamed of the extra money. He so needed a new pair of shoes. Maybe there'd even be enough for some new clothes for him and Mama and James. He was so ashamed of the poorness of his clothing. He imagined walking into Miss Miller's class with shiny new shoes, new pants and a crisp new shirt. He so wanted to look good for her.

CW refused to accompany Mama to Mr. Charlie's office for the settlement meeting. He couldn't bear to sit face to face with the man who had so mistreated him. Though his back problem had healed, his pride, what was left of it, was irreparably scarred. He went to work in the man's sawmill, took orders from him, but that was all.

Mama took Nate along with her, not wanting to go alone. She had hoped Teenie to go with her, but he had a rendezvous with his latest woman, a wild creature named Baby Doll. History had shown Mama that she could never count on Teenie, but she seemed always to forget. He hurt and disappointed her over and over, and she never learned to protect herself.

Mama and Nate waited in Mr. Charlie's office. After about a half hour he appeared. He rushed into the room without a hello and immediately pulled out a couple papers. Nate couldn't see what they said. He waited for the joyous news of the settlement. So certain he was that no butterflies danced in his stomach. He was perfectly calm even though he faced the man he hated most in the world.

Mr. Charlie looked up from his papers. "I see you brought the crazy little bastard boy with you," he said chuckling. "Bad seed, bad breeding." He laughed hard and began to cough. Pulling a white handkerchief from his pocket, he blew his nose loudly. As he put the rag back into his pants pocket, he looked directly at Nate and laughed out loud again. "I swear you niggers keep me so entertained when you aint driving me to drink."

Nate felt his face get hot. "It's all right," he told himself. "Just let him go on. The joke will be on him when he has to pay us."

Mr. Charlie shuffled his papers. Nate waited almost proudly for his announcement, but Mr. Charlie wasn't done tormenting them. He stared at Mama for what seemed like an eternity. "Don't you dare hurt her," Nate thought. "Pick on me. I can take it."

Mr. Charlie made a snorting sound through his nostrils and coughed. He never took his eyes off Mama. "Willie B, I swear you are the ugliest nigger I've ever seen," he drawled, "and that big ole knot on your forehead makes you look even uglier."

Nate jumped up. "My mama aint ugly. She beautiful."

Mama grabbed his arm pulling him back into his seat. She quietly shushed him. " I sorry, Mr. Charlie," she said. "Don't pay him no mind."

Mr. Charlie looked angrily at them, and then suddenly smiled.

"Whoa, watch out for the crazy boy. He belongs in a loony bin, I tell ya. And he'd be there if he weren't so damn good at pickin' my cotton."

Mama lowered her gaze and rocked slightly in her chair. "Yes, sir. Thank you, sir." She didn't want no trouble. All she wanted was to go home.

Suddenly, Mr. Charlie was all business, having had his fun. He stared at his yellow papers, going down the each sheet following with the point of a stubby pencil. "Willie B Lowe, you owe me thirty dollars for the use of my land. That is all," he announced, stood up from his desk and left.

Nate was stunned. Mr. Charlie hadn't even explained the numbers as he had in previous years. He was lying. He couldn't prove they owed, so he didn't bother to try. Mr. Charlie had lied. Nate was certain of it. There was no way that the family owed. Not when Nate had worked so hard and their quota had been so consistently met. Mr. Charlie was a liar and a cheat. And there was nothing his family could do about it.

"Let's go, child," Mama said almost immediately after Mr. Charlie left. She had taken the whole thing in stride and was not in the least upset.

"Mama, he lied. We don't owe no money. We made our quota. I know it."

Mama turned to her son. Her eyes blazed with anger. "You shut up right now," she said. She reached over and slapped Nate across the mouth.

Nate began to cry bitter tears. "Mr. Charlie's a liar," he yelled. "He nuthin' but a damn liar."

Mama slapped him again. "You shut up now," she said looking him straight in the eyes. Her voice was as strong and firm as he had ever heard. "I don't want to ever hear you say that again. Boy, you'll wind up dead sure as I'm standing here." She stormed out the door. Nate stood crying, confused and afraid for a few minutes then ran after her.

The two walked into the shack where CW was waiting for them. Mama told CW what had happened. He started yelling at Mama. "How the hell are we gonna pay that money?" he ranted.

"You and your good for nuthin' children gonna be the death of me. Can't even make the quota year after year. You a sorry excuse."

Mama began to cry. Nate stepped in to defend her. "He lied," Nate told CW. "We made our quota. I knows it."

CW turned to Nate. "Listen to the crazy good for nuthin'. You gonna get us all killed you keep sayin' that kinda thing."

Tears welled in Nate's eyes. "But…"

"Shut up," CW screamed. "Shut up."

He grabbed his had and coat. "This family will be the death of me yet." He started out the door. Mama ran after him, begging him not to leave, but he wouldn't come back.

Mama collapsed on the floor crying. She knew where he was going. She knew who he was going to see. Nate went over to her and tried to comfort her. "Get away from me," she told him. "James, come here and sit with your Mama." James, who had been playing all the while went over and sat by her. She threw her arms around him and sobbed. James glared at Nate as if to say, "Look what you've done."

Nate slipped out to the front porch and quietly went around to the back. He slid under the house and crouched in the chimney hole. Reaching into the pocket of his tattered coat, he pulled out the box Miss Miller had given him. He had taken it along to the settlement for good luck, but for him no luck could be found even with his teacher's blessing on him. He took out the red rubber ball and held it tightly in his hand. Quietly he sobbed. It was so cold his toes began to sting, but Nate stayed a long time before finally going inside and crawling into the stir mattress. He lay awake all night waiting for CW to come home, but he never returned that night.

Chapter Seven

Doll Baby was a crazy woman. She drank and smoked and caroused and could keep up with the men of the plantation on all counts. And she had a temper. The plantation folk knew better than to cross Doll Baby.

It was nearly inevitable that she and Teenie would become attracted to one another. Inevitable, but certainly unwise. At first the sexual chemistry was intoxicating, but soon the wars began. Plantation gossips had plenty to chatter about when Doll Baby and Teenie's stormy relationship played out publicly. Doll Baby was jealous by nature. Teenie, handsome and a snappy dresser, garnered much attention from the ladies—attention he could rarely resist.

The saloon was the backdrop for many a flagrant battle between the lovers. Teenie brought Doll Baby there to watch him jam on drums with the band. Women were constantly flirting with him, and a fight would ensue. Doll Baby would confront the would-be rival, shouting and screaming in her face. Teenie would throw down his drumsticks and come after her. The mess would end up with Teenie smacking Doll Baby and dragging her outside by her hair. A week later, the same thing would occur with a few minor variations.

"Why the hell does he bring her there? He knows they's gonna be trouble every damn time," Miss Pat said to her hen circle. "Oh Lord, I fear bad things ahead sure as I'm standin'."

The crescendo happened after an evening of drinking at a bar in Glen Allan. The fight started in the bar, and when Teenie went back to Doll Baby's house, the fight continued. Shouting and screaming went on for more than an hour. Teenie finally shoved

Doll Baby across the room and turned to walk out the door. She had enough of him. Her mind spinning she wanted only to finish it once and for all. She pulled a rusty switchblade from her purse. Running up behind him, she plunged the knife into his back between his shoulder blades with such force the blade broke off in his flesh.

Teenie was stunned, so much so he felt almost no pain. He turned around and glared at her. She stood across from him gripping the switchblade casing in her right hand. Teenie turned back around and walked through the door. It was finished.

Dazed, Teenie made his way to Mama's house. When she saw the wound with the blade stuck in it, Mama screamed. His shirt was soaked with blood. Mama managed to stop the bleeding, but was unable to remove the blade.

"Teenie, baby, you gotta go see a doctor," Mama begged, knowing her son too well. He refused to hear of it.

After three days walking around with the blade in his shoulder Teenie was gravely ill. He finally had no choice but to go to the hospital in Vicksburg. Doctors removed the blade and treated him for blood poisoning caused by the foreign object under his skin.

In the fall Nate would be moving into third grade at Chatham elementary school. He looked forward to the new school year with much anticipation. He worked hard all summer in the cotton fields. The Mississippi heat was intense often topping 100 degrees. Knowing his family's survival depended upon him, Nate persevered. The hard, hot earth baked his bare feet, which were slowly forming protective calluses over his young flesh. The sun scorched his back and his brow dripped with sweat. When many of the adults quit because the heat was too strong, Nate kept picking until the sun went down.

Folks on the plantation took notice of Nate's dedication to his family. A few of them took Mama aside and praised her son. Miss Pat especially recognized Nate's hard work and sacrifice.

"He's a good boy, Willie B," she told Mama one morning as they carried water back from the pump.

Mama just smiled at her. She was relieved when anyone noticed something good about her crazy son.

"How much you payin' him? Must be a good bit, he work so hard for it."

"I keeps all the money we get from Mr. Charlie. We need it for food and things."

"Why Willie B," Miss Pat exclaimed, "you oughta be ashamed. That boy deserves to be paid."

Mama's eyes widened with surprise. Miss Pat had never talked to her that way before. Mama thought about what Miss Pat had said. She wondered what the rest of the plantation would say behind her back after Miss Pat told them. She decided to give Nate 50 cents every Saturday out of the $35 the family made each week, due largely to his efforts.

At first Nate didn't want to take the money. But Mama insisted. She did not want to deal with the criticism she knew would follow if she did not pay her son. Finally, Nate agreed to accept the meager allowance.

The next day he found one of Big Mama's old Prince Albert tobacco cans. He dropped the shiny half dollar in, relishing the clank of metal against metal. He would save the money he made.

Soon the Prince Albert can was half full. Nate became obsessed with saving his coins. While the other boys spent their pennies at the plantation store, Nate would not. He watched them greedily devour penny candy and gulp soda pop. Nate was not jealous. Sometimes he allowed himself a treat or two, but he continued to hang onto the majority of what he earned. If Nate Lowe had a dollar he saved seventy-five cents without fail. If he saved his money going hungry was not thrust on him by a cruel twist of fate. It was his choice.

The school year had already begun, but there had not been a single day of rain. As he sat at lunchtime under a big old willow tree in front of the store, Nate occupied his mind praying for rain tomorrow. He gazed up at the sky. Not a single cloud floated above his head. But he knew not to give up hope. During the night a storm could blow up from the gulf and by morning the newly arrived clouds could burst and blessed rain would muddy the fields.

While folks milled around the storefront eating bits of food and resting for the afternoon's labor, Nate closed his eyes and dreamed of Miss Miller and the new wonders she'd soon be teaching him. He was so deep in his daydream that he didn't see the man standing in front of the store watching him. He was unaware of that man walking toward him, tentatively yet deliberately. "Boy..." the man said in a deep baritone voice.

"Huh?" Nate's eyes popped open. He stared up at the tall handsome man staring down at him through a pair of dark black sunglasses.

"What's your name, boy?"

"Nathaniel," Nate answered.

The man paused for a moment and then walked away as inexplicably as he had arrived.

As Nate watched the man go, he had an odd feeling. Who was he? What did he want? He began to feel afraid. Out of the corner of his eye, he saw Miss Pat approaching. Her face was serious. "Child, you know who that was?" she asked.

"Nope."

"That was your Daddy."

Miss Pat continued to talk, but Nate didn't hear a word. His Daddy. He felt numb, confused, and afraid. What if that strange man was planning to snatch him as Mama feared? Why did he reveal himself? Nate stood up suddenly leaving Miss Pat in mid-sentence. He went back to Mama's house and crawled underneath and sat in the chimney hole. There would be no more cotton picking today.

After a few hours Mama and CW began to call for him. Their cries became more and more angry. Nate had neglected his many chores. CW tried again. "Nate, where are you? Get inside, right now."

"I don't know where in hell he could be," Mama told her husband. "The house is a mess, we needs water. I'm gonna whoop him good when he gets home."

Nate listened as his Mama talked, but he didn't answer her calls. If he were going to be alone, it would be his choice. Not his Mama's and certainly not that stranger who was his Daddy.

Early the next morning Nate heard his favorite sound—raindrops pounding the roof of the shack. He smiled, as he lay awake stretched out at the end of the stir mattress. James slept next to him, and Mama snored on the other side of James. As sunlight came in through the shadeless window, Nate saw that CW was not on the bed once again. Nate knew Mama would wake up crying and continue sobbing as she struggled to get to Miss Ann's on time.

Nate dressed and waited to catch the school bus. After he returned from a trip to the outhouse, he watched Mama getting James ready for his first day of school.

"Oh Lord, you lookin' so handsome,' she told James as she straightened his shirt collar. "You such a big little man goin' to school. I can't hardly believe it."

James burst into tears. "Mama, I want to stay here with you. I don't wanna go to school," he cried.

Mama tried her best to convince James he'd like school, but James wouldn't hear of it. He sobbed all the way as Mama walked him and Nate up the road to the bus stop. Much to Nate's chagrin James cried the whole hour bus ride. Quite the opposite of his older brother, James would never like going to school.

Nate happily jumped off the bus and nearly sprinted into Miss Miller's room with the wailing James in tow. Miss Miller looked as pretty as ever in a crisp linen dress. She smiled at Nate. "Who do we have here?" she asked him.

"Oh, that's my little brother James," Nate said. "He don't wanna go to school."

Miss Miller crouched down and put her arm around James to comfort him. James squirmed away. She held out her hand to him. "Come. Let me show you something."

She took him over to the corner where a group of children were building a castle with wooden blocks. James's eyes lit up. He had never seen toys like that before. He started to build right along with the others, forgetting that he wanted to be home with his Mama.

Miss Miller walked back over to Nate. "Nathaniel, you're in the third grade this year.'

"Yes, ma'am," Nate said proudly.

"That means you're moving up at Chatham, and Miss Vaughn will be your teacher this year and next."

"But you're my teacher," Nate stammered. He was heartbroken. He struggled to keep from crying like his baby brother had.

"Come. You'll see. Miss Vaughn is nice and kind. She'll teach you lots of new things." She took Nate by the hand and led him into his new classroom.

Miss Vaughn met him and showed him to his desk. She was nice but not as pretty as Miss Miller. Nate began to feel a bit better, but he missed Miss Miller.

At lunch he saw her standing by the swings. He walked up to her. "Miss Miller."

"Yes, Nathaniel?"

"Can I come and visit you?"

Miss Miller looked down at him. "Nathaniel, you've got to move on. You're growing up and you got to go where that leads you."

"Yes, ma'am," Nate answered politely. He walked away very disappointed. He knew somehow she was right, but he also knew he'd never forget her kindness and thoughtfulness.

That Saturday Mom Pearl and Nate sat on the bank of the lake, fishing poles sinking in the murky water. A fish fry was planned for the next day and Nate volunteered to help his grandmother catch enough fish to feed the plantation folk who would soon be clamoring for her cooking. Nate was happy to spend the morning with Mom Pearl. She was one of the few people in his life who treated him with love and respect.

Today there was another reason Nate sought out Mom Pearl's company. He wanted to talk to her about meeting his father for the first time. He pulled his pole from the water and cast it in again, hoping to get lucky.

"Damn fish just aint bitin'," Mom Pearl complained. She put down her pole and pulled a tin of snuff from the pocket of her dungarees. She grabbed a pinch between her wizened fingers and shoved it into her mouth.

"Aww they'll be bitin' soon," Nate said, "They's just lazy this mornin'." Just then he felt a tug on his line. He jerked it back, digging the hook into fish flesh. The pulling became furious. He pulled back on the line and started to bring in his prize.

"Come on big fat fish. Mom Pearl want to fry you up and put you on a plate."

Mom Pearl laughed out loud. "Boy, you about to make me swallow my snuff." She helped Nate pull in the fish, a nice big one. "Now the spell's been broken. We gonna start some catchin'."

She was right. They caught fish after fish. Nate told Mom Pearl a school of fish must have been swimming upstream. He'd learned a lot about fish in Miss Vaughn's class. Mom Pearl listened intently to his discourse on fish behavior. She was impressed by how intelligent her grandson was. "You just keep on with school. You got the smarts for it. Don't you let nobody stop you," she told him proudly.

As the pair walked back to Mom Pearl's house, Nate found the courage to speak of his father. "My Daddy came up to me outside Mr. Charlie's store."

"Did he now?"

"Yes, ma'am he did. He asked my name and then he walked away. Miss Pat told me he was my Daddy."

Mom Pearl turned and looked at her grandson. She could see the pain on his face as he spoke. "That was all?"

"Uh huh."

They walked in silence for a few minutes. Then Nate spoke. "Mom Pearl, why doesn't he want to be my Daddy?"

She rubbed her forehead and spit some juice on the side of the trail. "They aint no accountin' for it. Just aint no accountin' for it." She stared off into the woods and felt like crying.

Neither of them spoke the rest of the way.

The following week tragedy revisited Nate's unlucky family. James was riding the swings in the school playground at recess. One of the boys in his class dared him to go higher and faster.

James pushed out hard with his legs and pulled back even harder with his arms. He felt like he was flying. A small crowd of children gathered to watch and urge him on. Suddenly, the boy on the swing next to him jumped off and the balance of the rusty metal swing set was upset. The front support legs jumped a few inches off the ground as James's swing flew backward. James struck his head on the retaining wall behind the swings. He fell to the ground unconscious. Teachers came running and carried him inside. He was taken to the hospital in Rolling Fork.

Nate was forgotten in the panic, and when the principal drove to the plantation to tell Mama what had happened she neglected to take him along. He went home on the school bus, not knowing if his brother was all right. He ran into the shack. Mama and CW were gone. Nate was terrified. His mind raced.

What if James was dead? Alone in the house, he sat down and cried. After awhile he fell asleep.

The sun was rising when he awoke. He found Mama and CW asleep on the stir mattress, but James was not there. "Mama," he screamed.

She awoke with a start. Her eyes were red and her face swollen.

Nate cried out again. "Where's James? Is he dead?"

Mama rubbed her eyes. "Shut up, you big baby. James is gonna be fine. We were scared for awhile, but he's gonna be all right."

"But where is he?"

CW stirred. "Tell that little bastard to be quiet," he shouted half awake.

Mama leaned toward Nate and whispered sternly, "The doctors said he had to stay at the hospital for a few days. Hush now and go to sleep."

Not even the news that his brother was okay could make Nate stop his crying. He gasped for air in between sobs.

Mama rolled over. "Shut up and go to sleep..."

Nate went back into the eating room and continued to softly cry.

When James came home from the hospital, he had a large bandage on the back of his head. He cried and whined a lot, and Mama and CW were right there to see to his every need. Both of them were traumatized by the thought that they might have lost their son. From then on they babied James even more than before, and James soon learned to take full advantage of their doting. Nate became even more invisible.

For a while CW came home every night after work. Mama seemed so happy once again. Nate took pleasure in seeing his Mama content after all the sadness he had seen her bear. But that peace was short lived. CW soon was back to his old ways, and Mama returned to quietly nursing a breaking heart.

Chapter Eight

When Nate was in the fourth grade, a total stranger profoundly affected his life. Dr. Martin Luther King's crusade for desegregation of Southern public schools was in full force. His movement was gaining nationwide support among oppressed black Americans and white liberals.

In Mississippi Dr. King's message was met with widespread fear. Whites were terrified their children would have to attend school with Negro children. In Nate's community whites pulled their children out of the white Chatham Elementary School and placed them in private schools to avoid having them mixed in with black children. In the sheltered world of the plantation most of the sharecroppers had barely even knew of Dr. King and his crusade to bring the American dream to Black Americans, but they would soon feel some of its effects.

The Blacks took over the abandoned white Chatham Elementary. Nate began the fifth grade at the more modern schoolhouse. Everything looked new—the blackboard, desks, easels, and shelves—the only exception being the textbooks. The Whites had taken their up to date textbooks with them, leaving the Black students to carry on in the out of date editions they used at the old school.

Dr. King's efforts brought the light of government attention to the plight of the children of sharecroppers. Soon plantation owners were informed that children had to be sent to school every day, not just when it rained. Opposition to the edict was fierce in the segregated South. A compromise was worked out in an effort to assuage the protests of the White population. Sharecropper children would be sent to school in the morning and dismissed at noon to return to the fields each afternoon.

It seemed like a dream to Nate. He could attend school every day. Miss Vaughn had taught his class about Dr. King and his work. Nate was amazed to discover that a Black man commanded such respect and wielded so much influence. It was a revelation. Dr. King became a role model for the young sharecropper child, who saw this great man as a symbol of the heights to which he aspired. Nate dreamed of meeting Dr. King someday.

The continuity of daily school attendance allowed Nate to begin to excel at his lessons. He was writing and reading. He devoured his textbooks and any other book he could get his hands on. His teachers began to view him as one of their best students. They were genuinely impressed by his drive and work ethic. His third and fourth grade teacher Miss Vaughn took a special interest in him that continued after Nate moved on to his new teacher. She prayed that God would give her student the opportunity to know the success he so deserved in spite of the tremendous obstacles that faced him.

While Nate rejoiced at daily school attendance, he also knew that his family's fortunes suffered as a result of his more limited time in the fields. He carried a lot of guilt and worry. He began to try to work well after twilight even when the moon was not full and shining. Without enough light, he learned to use his hands to feel the stalks and branches of the spindly cotton plants. Gently he would pinch the ends of the branches in search of boles. He learned to feel when the boles were plump and ready. It was not an exact science. He sometimes pulled off unripe puffs, but he soon became better at guessing the ripeness of the boles without using his eyes when the light was poor.

Of course, he could pick nowhere near as fast as he could during daylight, but his twilight haul of cotton did help. His after hours work kept the family close to meeting their quota every week. Without his extra efforts there would have been no hope of keeping up.

Still Mama fretted. She had so enjoyed the extra money Nate's work provided the family. Although there never seemed to be enough money for food and essentials, she worried less and counted on Nate more and more to fill in where the rest of the family failed. Some weeks when her worry got the better of her she'd send James, who hated school, and keep Nate behind to toil in the fields to make some extra money so that she could pay some on her tab at the store or purchase a chicken to fry on Saturday or buy some sugar to can the apples and peaches she picked from a trees on Tater Williams' plantation. After awhile Nate, at his mother's insistence, missed more and more days of school.

As he watched the sullen James ride off in the school bus, Nate's heart sank. Some days he fought back tears. There was an aching inside him to go, but he fought that desire. His devotion to his mother and her wishes was strong. Ironically, James was jealous of his brother for the first and only time of their childhood. Nate got to stay home while James had to suffer through a morning of school.

To pass the time in the fields and to raise his heavy heart, Nate sang as he chopped the cotton. The rhythm of the songs helped him keep a good pace while he worked. He sang at the top of his voice, loudly and proudly. There was a buzz around the fields about Nate's singing. The others stopped for a moment and listened as Nate belted out, "My baby don't have to worry, she don't have to rob and steal because I'm a driving wheel." Miss Pat was quick to point out to the others, "Oh yes sir, he just like his daddy, he is." The others nodded in agreement.

Nate's father was well known among plantation folk for being an excellent singer. At one time, the elder Nathaniel sang on the radio station in Greenville on Sundays. People expected that Nate would be an outstanding singer just like his father and Nate didn't disappoint them. Miss Pat took hold of his arm, looked him right in the eyes and said, "Child, you keep on singing. You got a gift from God." Miss Cheney, another of the old maids on the plantation and Miss Pat's housemate, nodded in agreement.

One Sunday morning bright and early Mr. Sylvester stopped by Mama's house to see Nate. Taken by the intelligent and talented young boy who lived his life without a father, Mr. Sylvester set his mind to helping the boy. Nate had gone to church with him only a few times since he sang for the congregation. Picking cotton for his family became more important than church. Mr. Sylvester knew this, but did not agree. To him the boy's salvation was most important, and he hatched a plan to ensure that Nate would come to church more regularly.

"Morning, Mr. Syl," Nate said, coming out onto the porch to greet him.

"Morning, boy."

The two stood and stared off at the horizon for a few minutes. Then Mr. Syl spoke. "I'm goin' to church this mornin'. Want to come along?"

Nate smiled. "Why yes, I sure do. Let me ask Mama." He called into the house.

"Go on," Mama answered, "but you gots to do your chores first."

Mr. Syl chuckled. "You do your chores. I'll come back by fer ya."

Nate raced through his chores, washed up and put on his nicest pair of khaki pants and a brown button down shirt. His shoes were dull and tattered, but he shined them up as well as he could. He told Mama he'd pick cotton after he came home. Mama reluctantly agreed. She didn't like him going to church, especially when the family needed him.

Nate waited on the porch listening to Mama complaining about him. "Too big for his britches that boy," she said loud enough for Nate to hear. "Thinks he too good for us. Goin' off to church. Leavin' his Mama alone with all this work." As he listened Nate began to think he shouldn't go to church. Maybe Mama was right. She needed him and he was abandoning her. Just then he saw Mr. Syl rounding the bend to his house.

"Let's get goin'," he said. We got just enough time to get to the church before the preacher starts a-preachin'."

"I don't know, Mr. Syl. I think Mama needs me here," Nate said.

Mr. Syl saw the pained look on the boy's face and recognized his turmoil. "Look here," he told Nate. "If you visit the Lord's house regular, He will send his blessings to you and your family. He will help you now and in the future in ways you can only imagine. That's the Lord I know and the Lord I want you to know."

A smile crossed Nate's lips. "Yes, Mr. Syl," he said, "I want to know Him, too."

"Well let's go then," Mr. Syl replied, putting his arm around Nate's shoulders. The two set off together walking the three miles to Pleasant Star church.

The church itself was inside an old wooden building with a tar roof and a few windows. The interior was sparse with rows and rows of chairs with sea grass seats. The seats were hand made by members of the congregation out the material that was used to tie up hay bales. At the front of the church were two special seats where the deacons sat and behind them was the pastor's podium. Behind the podium stood the choir. The church was full and alive with the faithful talking and laughing. Nate and Mr. Syl made there way down the aisle and sat on the inside end of a row of seats very close to the front.

Many people stopped and said hello to Mr. Syl. He was obviously very well known at Pleasant Star and very well liked. Nate felt proud to be with such a prominent man. The pastor stood up and raised his arms up in the air and the people quickly sat down and became silent. The choir stood up and sang. The beauty of their music enthralled Nate. Down in front, Miss Minnie Barksdale played an old upright piano that was always out of tune, but she managed just fine.

The pastor began to speak on the lesson of the day. Nate listened intently. Intermittently people in the crowd called out in agreement with the pastor's words. The energy was electric. Nate loved the way church felt.

The pastor began to make his way down the aisle as he spoke. He stopped right next to Nate's seat. Little Nate craned his neck to look up at him.

"People, we got a brother here who has a gift from God for singing," the pastor said as he looked down at Nate. "We need to get behind him and push him to succeed." He smiled at Nate with a look of pride. Nate felt very honored by his attention.

"Brother Lowe, come up here and sing a song for us." The congregation, many of whom had heard Nate's singing in the fields, shouted out their encouragement.

Nate looked at Mr. Syl, who was grinning proudly back at him. Nate realized the whole thing was a set up and he couldn't have been more grateful to his friend. Without a speck of fear Nate rose from his seat and walked up to Miss Minnie Barksdale at the piano. This time he was confident, more practiced and his voice had grown stronger. "I'm gonna sing "There Will Be No Tomorrow When Jesus Comes." She nodded and began to play.

As he looked out of the congregation a feeling of pure joy rose up from his belly, and Nate sang better than he had ever sang before. Unlike the last time, his eyes were open the entire time. He looked up to the ceiling as though he were singing to God then down to the congregation as if to share God's blessing with them. When he was done, the people rose to their feet praising the Lord and one of their own that shined so brightly among them.

It wasn't long after that Nate was singing at Pleasant Star or Guiding Star or some other plantation church nearly every Sunday. He joined the choir at Pleasant Star. Miss Mathilda Griffin was the president of the choir and she fell in love with his talent and soon took the young boy under her wing as his reputation grew and grew.

Each day when she checked over the school attendance cards and found Nate Lowe absent, Miss Vaughn was sorely disappointed. She had seen it before. A promising student derailed by the demands of the suffocating sharecropper existence. Nate was as special as any of those past students. He deserved a better chance at reaching his potential. As she closed the attendance books and watched her class struggling with a surprise quiz in long division, Miss Vaughn knew she had to do something to help Nate.

One day after school, Miss Vaughn drove out to Mr. Charlie's plantation and after quite a bit of walking and asking around she found Mama in the field. Mama was taken aback by the sudden appearance of Nate's teacher. She looked askance at Miss Vaughn, wondering what she could possibly want.

"I'm here to talk about your son and the fact that he's missing so much school," Miss Vaughn said.

Mama smiled shyly. "Well, I needs him here to work."

"I understand, but he's such a promising student with such potential."

Mama didn't quite know what to say. "But, ma'am, he's good at workin' the fields, and that's all he needs."

Miss Vaughn tried to convince Mama that Nate could move beyond life on the plantation with the right education and encouragement. Mama did not believe nor understand. She could not conceive of life outside the plantation for herself or her son. Miss Vaughn quickly recognized Mama's shortsightedness, but she was able to extract from her a promise to send Nate to school more. For a time, Mama followed through on her word to Nate's teacher.

Around this time another big change occurred in Nate's life, this time much closer to home. Mama's marriage to CW had deteriorated almost beyond repair. CW was cheating on her constantly and had been for years. The brief guilty period following James's accident had long since ended and the two had drifted far apart. CW barely ever stayed at the family house anymore. One afternoon he stopped by to see Mama and told her he was leaving to go into the army. Mama, who still loved her husband, was devastated. She burst into hysterical crying. CW, weak man that he was, couldn't bear the guilt of seeing her cry, so he told her it was for the good of their marriage, that they needed time apart, that when he returned in three years at the end of his enlistment, they could work on getting back together. Mama believed him, but still felt sad and alone. In reality, CW had joined the army to escape his marriage. He was not strong enough to end it outright.

A few weeks after CW unceremoniously left for the army, there was a knock at Mama's door one evening. Mama went to the door and said, "Who is that?"

A booming voice answered, "It's Lee Bell. Open the door."

"What do you want?"

"Don't ask what I want, just open the door."

Nate walked over and stood behind Mama as she waited wondering whether or not to let Lee inside. Nate didn't like Lee Bell. He was dingy looking, tall and sloo footed. He had buckteeth and white stuff was always coming out of the corners of his mouth. He seemed always to be talking about sex. When he saw him coming Nate tried to hide because he didn't want to hear what that nasty man had to say. Lee Bell was married to Clara and he mistreated her badly.

Nate touched Mama on the shoulder and was about to tell her not to let him in, when Mama opened the door.

Lee Bell entered abruptly. He stood there dressed in a plaid shirt, dirty jeans and boots covered in mud. As Nate surveyed him he had a bad feeling. Then his eyes fell on the shotgun in Lee Bell's right hand.

"Get on in the room," he commanded Mama. She stood frozen for a moment and then she walked into the sleeping room. Lee Bell turned to follow.

Nate ran up behind him. "What are you gonna do to my Mama," he demanded.

"Shut up boy, or I'll hit you over the head with my gun."

Nate realized in an instant Lee Bell was serious. He shrank back and went over and sat with James.

From the other room Nate heard his mother crying. "Lee, please don't do it."

"Shut up, bitch. Don't make me hurt you."

Nate listened helplessly to his mother being raped. Mama cried and begged Lee Bell to stop. Nate didn't know what to do. He was scared and his mind was racing. He though of taking a big stick and beating Lee Bell over the head with it, but he was afraid Lee Bell would shoot him or worse yet Mama.

James was too young to understand what was going on; Nate was barely old enough to comprehend himself. James was tired so Nate laid him down on some blankets on the floor and he was soon asleep. Nate was not so lucky. He couldn't fall asleep with the sound of Mama sobbing in the other room. He pulled a blanket over his head and cried.

After a while Nate heard Lee Bell leave through the back door. Mama came into the room and lay down on the floor by the window. She was still crying. Nate kept the cover over his head. He wanted to go over and comfort her, but he was afraid.

In the morning Mama said nothing of what had happened the night before. She never told anyone and neither did Nate.

The matter was never spoken of again. If Mama had spoken out, no one would have had any concern of sympathy for her. The men on the plantation would have assumed the raped woman asked for it. Plantation women had learned not to speak of rape. That was just the way it was.

A few days after the rape Mama decided to give up her house and move in with Big Mama while CW was away. The time spent with CW gone and his family living with his grandmother was dark years for Nate. He focused more than ever before on his studies. He had finished his years in Miss Vaughn's class and moved on to finish fifth and sixth grades with Chatham principal, Miss Agnes Williams as his teacher. Miss Williams was not like Miss Miller or Miss Vaughn. She was more strict and demanding of her students. It was during his years in Miss William's class that Nate began to keep more to himself. The weight of his home life began to take its toll and weighed more and more on his psyche.

During his residence in Big Mama's house, Nate increased his work in the fields as well. He was most happy when he was not at home, so he set about seeing that he was there as little as possible. Work was a logical outlet for him. Soon he began to work in the evenings on neighboring plantations when the boss men found themselves shorthanded. Nate was a hot commodity; his skill at cotton picking was well known. Neighboring plantation owners were only too happy to pay him a few dollars to help them harvest. Mr. Charlie was quick to warn his peers, "Ahhh, don't treat that one the wrong way. The boy's plum crazy, I tell ya."

After a morning of learning and a whole day of working in the fields at home and away, Nate stumbled home to Big Mama's house with just enough energy to lie down and fall asleep. He arose and was out of the house in the morning before anyone else stirred. No one saw him, no one got the chance to speak to him, no one could blame him, and no one could beat him.

Chapter Nine

As Nate worked in the field carefully chopping the infant cotton plants to encourage the stronger plants to grow, he couldn't stop thinking about his sorry lot in life. He felt like he was cursed, like misfortune was his birthright. He began to doubt his dream of ever finding a way off the plantation. The boy without a father, the boy who was beaten and blamed, the boy who was never loved and appreciated was beginning to crumble under the strain.

Later that evening Nate wandered down to the store after dark. Carl Lee, Jimmy Lee and Phillip, a couple of men from the plantation, were loitering outside drinking corn whiskey. Carl Lee said hello to Nate and offered him a drink from a brown bottle. Nate accepted. The liquid burned as it went down, but shortly after Nate began to feel good. He laughed and talked and joked with his cohorts.

"Boy, you sure is funny," Carl Lee exclaimed. He laughed and laughed watching Nate get more and more drunk. Carl Lee thought watching a pre-adolescent boy stumble about and nearly fall over was the most amusing thing he'd seen in a long time.

After a few hours, Carl Lee made sure Nate got back home safely. He led Nate inside and laid him down on the stir mattress. Mama was fast asleep and didn't notice anything, not even a few hours later when Nate awoke and ran outside to vomit.

The next morning Nate had a terrible hangover, but he remembered how good he felt when he was drinking and he wanted more. He recalled that Teenie had brought some Orange Driver to the house a few nights before. When Mama left to work at Miss Ann's, Nate opened a bottle and took a long drink. It tasted like orange soda and felt so good going down. He took another swig. That calm and happy feeling began to return. Nate relaxed. When the bottle was half empty, Nate got the water jug and filled the bottle back up to the top. Teenie would never know.

Of course, it didn't take long for Teenie to discover that his drink had been watered down. He knew who the culprit was right away, but he went easy on his little brother. Nate didn't even get a beating for what he had done.

From then on Nate knew he had to get his own. He began to use some of the saved money he'd buried in the old Prince Albert can and bought a couple of bottles of Orange Driver or Morgan Davis, which tasted like grape juice, for fifty cents a bottle at Mr. Charlie's store. When the weekend came, Nate was drunk every Friday and Saturday. On Sunday he sobered up and was clear headed to go back to work and school on Monday. By his twelfth year Nate had found a new way to escape from his life.

In the fall Nate began classes at Moore Middle School. In the new building with new teachers and many unfamiliar students Nate felt especially alone. When he was at home, he barely noticed Mama cry when Big Mama went on and on about how Mama had driven CW away and what losers both of them were. He began to shut everyone out. At school he was quiet and kept to himself. At lunch he sat at the long tables with his head down on the cool varnished wood table, and no one noticed. Except for one day.

"This seat taken?" a voice said to him.

Nate barely heard the voice.

"Excuse me..."

Nate raised his head and squinted his eyes. A short boy in a crisp plaid shirt, lunch tray in hand looked down at him. "Yeah?"

"I said, is this seat taken?"

Nate motioned toward the other side of the table. "Nah, go ahead."

The boy sat down directly across from him. What the hell does he want, Nate said to himself, annoyed by the intrusion into his world. After a few minutes he sat up and stared at the boy who had so rudely invaded. He watched the boy eating his hash and cornbread. He was so neat and proper. He wiped the corner of his mouth with his paper napkin and chewed with his mouth ever so tightly closed. The boy picked up his milk carton and took a long drink.

"Lionel Jenkins, pleased to meet you," he said thrusting his right hand in Nate's direction.

Nate was too foggy to respond quickly. After a couple of seconds, he reached out and shook the boy's hand. "Nate Lowe," he replied.

After lunch the boys sat along the school wall, waiting for the bell to ring. Lionel was from town. He talked of a life Nate had never known, one of stores and shops, and libraries, and jobs and opportunities. It was foreign to Nate, but he wanted to know more. Lionel was a nice boy, serious about school, polite and kind to everyone he met. Nate wanted to be more like Lionel. Soon the two boys were friends and began spending more and more time together at school.

Lionel wanted Nate to come to his house in town. Nate always made some excuse. He knew if he went to Lionel's house it would, of course, be inevitable that he'd have to invite Lionel to his home. Nate never wanted to have to do that. He was too ashamed of his home and his life and the people in it.

But nothing would stop their friendship. Nate began to call his friend Chip, for no particular reason, but Lionel understood that Nate's assigning him a nickname was the highest praise Nate could bestow on him.

Chip's parents lived about a block from Moore Elementary School in Glen Allan. His father was a mechanic. Since his family wasn't dependent on the whims of a plantation owner, Chip always had some pocket change, which he gladly shared with his friend. Chip made money by helping his father fix cars. When the two boys were out and about walking in the city, Chip would give his buddy a quarter so Nate could buy a Baby Ruth bar and a root beer. Chip was naturally generous and thought nothing of it.

Oftentimes Nate would miss school days to work in the fields. When he returned to school, Chip would sit with him before and after school and at lunch not satisfied until Nate was completely caught up with the lessons he had missed.

"Okay, now we got you right with history," Chip said sounding very serious and businesslike, "but this English lesson on punctuation is tough. I don't think I understand it my damn self."

The two boys looked at each other and laughed out loud. Their laughter caught the attention of a group of city boys who were leaning against the wall next to them.

"Look at that farm nigger, thinking he's smart," one of the boys called over.

"Yeah, go on back to the farm, nigger. You don't belong here."

Nate stared at the ground. His face grew hot with anger.

One of the boys walked up and stood in front of him. "You got somethin' to say to us, nigger?"

Chip grabbed Nate by the arm and led him away from the trouble. Nate was humiliated. He wondered why Chip would want to be friends with someone so different and disadvantaged. He was sure that Chip would abandon him, and he wouldn't blame him.

"Look at me, Nate."

Nate raised his gaze to meet his friend's. To his surprise, Chip was smiling. "What are you worried about?" he said. "That boy's getting an F in math. He's dumb as a post. You're way smarter than him."

Nate still couldn't shake the bad feeling in his stomach.

"Listen," Chip continued, "you remember last week when Mr. MacBeth came into class and was askin' kids to recite their times tables?"

"Yeah," Nate said a smile already beginning to appear on his lips.

"What happened when he asked that boy to say his 3 times table?"

Nate raised his hand to his forehead and giggled.

"Come on, you know. What happened?"

"He got stuck on three times three." Nate hardly got the words out before the two boys nearly collapsed in laughter.

Chip put his hand on Nate's shoulder. "Son, you're way better and smarter than all them. Don't let them bother you."

As they made their way back to class after lunch, Nate heard someone calling his name. He turned to see a teacher hurrying to catch up with him. An imposing woman, she was tall about five foot ten and large about one hundred eighty pounds. He expected she was a teacher he hadn't met yet. But why was she following him? Had he done something wrong, he wondered. He wasn't quite sure how things were done in this big school, so he reasoned he could easily broken some rule or another. He stopped so she could catch up to him.

She was slightly out of breath when she reached him, but she smiled. It was a pleasant smile with bright and white with a gold filling between her front teeth. She reached out her hand to shake Nate's. "I'm Mrs. Miller the music teacher."

Nate shook her hand, noticing her finely groomed nails that were polished a bright red. "Nate Lowe," he said sheepishly, still wondering what he had done.

She pushed back her wire-framed glasses. "I hear you are quite a talented singer."

Nate was a bit embarrassed. "Well…"

Mrs. Miller smiled. "Don't be modest," she laughed. "Would you sing for me if I played the piano?"

Nate looked around all of the other students had gone into their classrooms where he should have been. "Right now?"

"Sure and don't worry I'll write you an excuse."

"All right," Nate said.

The two walked toward the music room. Nate had never seen anything like it. There were chairs and music stands and a few instruments here and there. A director's baton rested on the podium in the front. It wasn't a large room, but it was a whole room devoted to music. Up front sat a spinet piano. Mrs. Miller went over to it and sat down at the keys. "You stand here on the side of the piano facing me."

Nate obliged, but felt a bit awkward. He wasn't used to singing anywhere but church or in the fields.

"Stand up straight, son. You're collapsing your diaphragm."

Nate looked puzzled. "What's a diaphragm?"

"Why it's the muscle that controls your breathing and pushes the notes out of your throat." She got up from the piano, came over and pushed lightly at the top of his belly. "It's right here. Try clenching it and moving it in and out."

"Oh," Nate said. "I can feel it pushing up against my ribs."

"Exactly," she said. "If you can learn to make that muscle stronger and control your breathing, you'll be an even better singer that I hear you are."

Nate marveled at this newfound part of his body. He had no idea of how his singing worked. He just sang and let it come as it would. He had no idea he could actually work to make his singing better. "You mean it?" he asked almost innocently.

"Absolutely," she answered confidently, "and I can help you learn, but first let me hear you."

Nate began to feel more comfortable. He knew his voice was good enough and he wanted to impress Mrs. Miller so she would teach him all she knew about singing.

"What would you like me to play?"

Nate stood confidently by the piano. "I sing church music."

Mrs. Miller chuckled. "Then church music it is."

Miss Miller began to play a "He is Sweet, I Know" a song Nate had sung many times before in church. He shut his eyes and belted out the hymn. Mrs. Miller fell in love with his voice right then and there. She was thrilled by his talent, and encouraged him to sit in on as many of her music classes as he could and to join the school chorus. From that moment, Nate became her favorite and most prized student of all.

When Nate came home from school that day, Mama called him. "Boy, you go pack up your things. We movin'."

Nate was astonished. "Where we goin'?"

"Mr. Charlie give us another house."

Nate couldn't help but shout out a hooray. Big Mama, who was sitting on her porch, heard him. "Yeah, nigger, you go on. See how long y'all makes it without Big Mama lookin' out for y'all. You and your good for nuthin' Mama."

Mama looked as though she was about to cry. "Mama, don't you pay her no mind. We gonna be just fine," Nate said.

Mama forced a smile, but Nate could see the worry on her face.

Big Mama had a great influence over her, and Mama shuddered as she wondered if she could make it on her own.

"You go on now, boy. Pack up your things. We gonna make it on our own. Or die tryin'."

Nate threw his arms around his mother's neck. He was so proud of her in that moment. The strength she had mustered to strike out on her own was uncharacteristic but so welcome. He knew how hard it was for her to disobey Big Mama's wishes.

As Mama, Nate and James were ready to leave with their belongings in tow, Big Mama grabbed hold of Mama's arm. "Why don't you leave James here with me? I can't see you messin' with that precious boy. He too good to be raised by the likes of you."

A rare shot of anger at her mother flared in Mama. She pulled her arm away. "No. I's taken my baby with me. He belongs with his Mama." With that Nate's family walked out of Big Mama's house.

Chapter Ten

The new house was another shack on Mr. Charlie's plantation the fourth one the family had lived in since Nate was born. Whenever Mr. Charlie needed a bigger house for a growing sharecropper family, it seemed Mama was the first one he ordered to move to another smaller dwelling. The house he had given Mama this time was more undesirable than the last. It was a shotgun house—walk in the front door and walk through all the rooms in a straight line to the back door. It was one of the lowliest on the entire plantation. As Nate pulled his few belongings out of a brown paper sack and hung them on a rope line in the sleeping room, he cursed Mr. Charlie. He was sure that despite the meagerness of the house Mr. Charlie would once again demand a settlement at the end of December.

Mama was not at all disappointed with her new home. She sang out loud as she swept the floors, approaching the move out from under Big Mama's wing with blind optimism. "Wait till CW gets back and sees our new house," she said as she moved the old wooden table into place. "He gonna love it." Nate felt pleased to see her so happy. He was happier still that he wouldn't have to live in Big Mama's house anymore.

A knock came at the screen door. Nate went to answer. To his surprise, Carl Lee was standing in the doorway, a sheepish grin on his face.

"Hello, Nate," Carl Lee said.

"Carl Lee, afternoon…"

"Pretty day, aint it?

"Yeah, it is. Listen, we just moved in here and I gots to help

Mama. Can't go down to the store tonight." Nate assumed Carl Lee had stopped by to see if Nate would be joining the boys who would invariably spend the evening drinking down by the store.

Carl Lee started to laugh. "Oh, nah, boy. I aint here for you. I come for your Mama."

Just then Mama came in from the back of the house. "Carl Lee, you early. I aint near ready."

"You lookin' mighty fine to me," Carl Lee told her.

Nate's heart sank. He had no idea Mama was seeing Carl Lee. CW had only been away a little over a year and Mama was already cheating. And only a few minutes before Mama had been talking about CW's return. When he thought about it, the whole thing made sense, though. Big Mama was always preaching to Mama she needed to find herself a man. CW was no good. He left her. Why should she be alone? She needed a man to take care of her.

Even in her stab at independence, Mama was still controlled by Big Mama. Nate knew she loved CW and left to her own devices she would have waited for him to return from the army, but Big Mama's influence was just too strong. Mama's will was too weak.

As Mama and Carl Lee left for the juke house, Mama was giggling like a schoolgirl. Nate found a bottle of cheap Morgan Davis he had hidden and went down to the lake bank and drank alone until he passed out.

After that Carl Lee was a frequent visitor. Sometimes he stayed the night. Sometimes he brought Mama a plucked chicken or a bag of potatoes. When Nate saw Carl Lee around the plantation, he always said nice things about Mama. He never had a bad word to say about her. Nate began to think that Carl Lee was good for his Mama. But still Nate was confused about how to act around him. He wasn't his stepfather even though he was around the house so much. Could he tell Nate what to do like a Daddy did? Did Nate have to obey him if he did? Would Carl Lee give him a beating if Nate didn't obey? Nate's confusion caused him to withdraw. He didn't want to say anything that might upset Mama. He didn't want her to know of his confusion and tacit disapproval, so he said nothing.

James, Nate realized, stood to be even more confused than he was. Fortunately, James appeared oblivious to the puzzling relationship, so absorbed was he by his own interests and pursuits. For extra measure, Nate shielded James. Whenever Mama and Carl Lee looked like they were getting amorous, Nate coaxed James outside to play or distracted him with a new game or toy Nate had made for him.

On Sunday Mrs. Miller came to pick up Nate to take him to a church in far off Louise, Mississippi. "Mrs. Lowe, your son sings like an angel," Mrs. Miller told Mama. "Why don't you come with us?"

Mama brushed one of her braids back from the side of her face. "Oh, naw. I'm not dressed for church." She motioned down toward her dirty overalls.

"We got time. How about we wait for you to get dressed?" Nate watched his mother for her reply, hoping she'd say yes. Mama had never seen him sing in church.

"Naw, you go on. I gots work to do here."

Disappointed Nate turned toward the door. "All right then," said Mrs. Miller, "you don't know what you'll be missin'."

The church in Louise was huge. Nate was awestruck. Mrs. Miller shepherded him up to the pews on the side of the pulpit. She went off and talked to some well-dressed old ladies and pointed back at Nate. One of the ladies in a blue and white polka dotted dress came up and asked Nate what he wanted to sing. She told him she would raise up her right hand when it was time for him to stand up to sing. Nate nodded that he understood.

The church filled up quickly. There must have been two hundred people. The polka dot lady sat down at the piano and began to play. The people were silent. When she was done, the preacher stepped up to the pulpit, which was an old wooden lectern. He was a gray haired man in the black suit with a beautiful satin scarf around his neck that hung down past his belt and had an embroidered gold cross on each end. His voice, a low baritone, boomed throughout the church. He spoke about the Lord's commandment and the Lord's desire to preserve the family. "The sin of adultery is the gravest sin of all to the family," he said, "and the Lord looks harshly upon adulterers."

Nate began to have a sick feeling in his stomach. "Sinners, cast out the demon of adultery. Repent and be healed," the preacher told the congregation. "The Lord will heal you."

Nate thought about Mama. She was sinning with Carl Lee while her husband was away. "But if you do not, the Lord will have vengeance upon you. You will be cast into Hell to live a life of eternal Hell fire and damnation."

A stinging fear gripped Nate. He feared for his Mama. Would she be sent to Hell when she died for the life she was leading? Lost in his thoughts, Nate didn't see the polka dot lady raise her hand. She saw that Nate wasn't looking at her so she stood up and waved her hand in the air till she got his attention. Nate stood up. The music began and he sang. He sang from the depths of his heart all the while praying that the Lord would take his offering of his song and spare his Mama. He looked up at the ceiling toward God as he always did, but this time he asked God to show mercy on his Mama. He sang his best, hoping God would accept his gift and save Mama.

After the service, Mrs. Miller was beaming as several old ladies approached her asking about her young prodigy. She called Nate over to the group. Reluctantly he joined them. He didn't much like the way the old ladies invariably fawned over him. It made him uncomfortable to be praised.

In the car on the way back to the plantation, Mrs. Miller couldn't stop talking about Nate's performance. "Child, that was the best you ever sang," she told him. "I never had a student that could sing as good as you. Your talent is a gift from the Lord that will take you very far if you keep on singing."

Nate sat quietly. He would be truly happy if his singing would take him and Mama far, far away from Mr. Charlie's plantation.

Winter was approaching quickly and the last of the cotton soon was picked. Nate had a lot of time on his hands. He began to spend more and more of his pocket change on liquor and more and more of his weekend time was spent in an alcohol haze.

One November evening he was staggering home from a few hours of sipping Orange Driver by the lake bank. He saw a dark figure walking toward him. He squinted his eyes to try to make out who it was. As he focused on the distant figure, he didn't see a rock sticking out of the ground. He tripped on it and fell to the ground. Before he knew it there was a hand under his arm helping him up.

He struggled to get to his feet as fast as he could, but his limbs weren't cooperating and he fell down again.

"Whoa, there, boy." It was Teenie who had just been to the house to visit Mama. Teenie laughed out loud. Nate looked up at him. He couldn't understand what was so funny. "Boy, you is drunker than a skunk." Teenie couldn't stop laughing.

"So," Nate said, pulling his arm away.

"Teenie, what the hell's goin' on out there?" Mama yelled from the front porch.

Nate and Teenie looked at each other for a moment. Just as Nate was about to beg his brother not to tell Mama he was drunk, Teenie yelled, "Nuthin', Mama. Just me and Nate talkin'. Go on back inside."

"Oh, all right. Tell Nate to get in here. He's got chores."

Teenie waited the low squeak and bang of the screen door shutting and then he burst into laughter again. "Boy, you don't look like you be doin' any chores tonight."

"Shut up, Teenie," Nate said. His brother's teasing didn't amuse him.

"Come on, boy, get on up to your feet." Nate followed his brother's direction and stood up. His head was spinning.

"I'll go back on in with you and tell Mama's you's sick so you don't have to do no chores."

Nate looked at his brother with surprise. Teenie had never stood up for him or helped him before. In his brother's eyes he thought he saw love for the first time. Even in his stupor he saw it plainly. Tears welled up in his eyes. So long had he waited for approval from his older brother.

Teenie took Nate by the arm and led him to the house. Just as they were about to step onto the porch, Teenie stopped, looked down at his brother and said, "Boy, you all right. I gots to take you drinkin' with me and the boys sometime." He got Nate into the sleeping room and laid him down on the bed. It wasn't long before Nate passed out.

A couple of weeks later Teenie was good to his word. He came to Mama's and found Nate sitting on the porch. Nate had forgotten his key and he was waiting for Mama to come home and let him inside.

"Why don't you come along with me?" Teenie asked.

"Nah, I gots chores to do."

"Aww, come on, boy. All you ever do is work and go to school. You gots to get out and have some fun."

Nate reluctantly agreed to go along. He got in to Teenie's old black car. He slid across the gray vinyl seats making a squeaking sound. "This is nice, Teenie."

"Aww, it's all right." Teenie said. "I'm fixin' to get me a convertible. Now that's a sweet machine."

Teenie was headed to a juke house called the Green Frog, but first he stopped and hung out at a couple of his friends' houses. Nate was quickly becoming bored with the scene. After a while the crew crammed into Teenie's car and drove to the juke house. Teenie's friends were loud and crass. One guy belched loudly and laughed hysterically each time. Teenie's driving was erratic down the dirt road. Nate suspected he'd had more than a few drinks. Every time Teenie skidded off the road the whole gang shouted "whoooaa" and laughed. Nate didn't see what was so funny.

The juke house was crowded and smoky. Several of Teenie's friends came over as soon as they walked in. "What's happenin', Teenie?"

"Hey, Philip."

"I see you brought your little bro', man, that's cool. What's happenin' lil' bro." Philip raised his hand in the air and Nate met it with his in a high five.

"Come on, Nate, let's get us some booze. What you say?"

Nate, a little bewildered by all the people and the noise, felt uncomfortable and tired. "I'm gonna wait outside in the car."

Nate fought his way through the crowd and outside. He opened the car door and jumped into the back seat. Soon he fell asleep. After a couple hours he awoke cold and shivering. He was freezing. Surveying the front of the juke house he saw no sign of Teenie. He waited, his teeth chattering. He tried to huddle on the floor between the front and back seats for warmth, but still he was cold.

After a time, he began to get angry, and he opened the car door and headed back into the juke house.

The Green Frog was a house painted green on the outside. People milled about the rooms, smoking and drinking, flirting and talking. A dance floor was set-aside in the back room and in the corner was a space where the band set up. Teenie often played drums in the pick up band that formed for the evening's entertainment. In the kitchen was a counter where drinks were served. Mostly beer was sold, but the owner Miss Annie also offered wine, white lightening, rum homebrew, and corn whiskey. Sometimes Miss Annie sold food like fried catfish, too. Next to the store, the Green Frog was the most popular place on the plantation. Everyone went there. Now that he had been there, Nate wondered what all the fuss was about. All he saw was a bunch of people he would rather avoid. He preferred to do his drinking alone.

After wandering for half an hour through the rooms and squeezing by one drunken reveler after another, he finally found his brother. He tugged on Teenie's sleeve to get his attention. "I'm tired. I wanna go home."

Teenie turned slowly around to face Nate. He looked angry. He was deeply involved in convincing a young lady to take him home that night. She had her arm around his neck. "You wanna go home. The night is just startin', boy. We can't leave now."

The lady on his shoulder, pinched Nate's cheek. "What a cute little boy," she cooed.

Nate shrugged off her attention. Teenie turned his back on him and returned his attention to the lady of the moment.

Nate went back out to the car. He rested his head against the window and tried to fall asleep, but he was too damn mad. How could his brother do this to him? He stormed back inside and demanded Teenie's car keys so that he could turn on the heater. Teenie turned over the keys and shooed Nate away. Nate was cramping his style.

Nate had no intention of using the heater. He was going to start the car and drive himself home. He didn't care what happened to Teenie. He just wanted to go home and go to bed.

He stuck the key into the ignition and turned over the motor. The car whined and wouldn't start.

Back inside, Philip who had just been outside, walked quickly up to Teenie. "Hey, Teenie."

Aggravated by another interruption, Teenie shouted, "What you want, man?"

Philip was taken aback. "Hey, man, I just thought you should know, lil bro's tryin' to start your car, that's all."

"God damn it." Teenie raced outside. He opened the car door. "Slide over, you little bastard."

Nate obeyed. He hardly cared that Teenie was angry. Teenie reached over and thumped him on the head. "Man, I thought you was cool," he said smacking Nate's head again. "But you just a drag, man. A real drag."

"Shut up, Teenie. Just take me home." Nate couldn't believe he had spoken so boldly to his brother, but the odd thing was Teenie seemed to respect Nate standing up for himself. He didn't say another word to his little brother the entire way.

As they drove up to Mama's house the sun was just peeking over the horizon. Nate vowed that he'd never go out with his brother again.

Chapter Eleven

His first concert. And the church was packed. Standing room only. Nate sang ten songs all by himself without a choir behind him. Mrs. Miller played piano for him. Afterward Nate was beaming. He couldn't wait to tell Mama. People had come to Pleasant Star just to hear him sing. Miss Mathilda Griffin said Nate had the most beautiful singing voice she had ever heard, and Minnie Barksdale had tears in her eyes as she told him she felt the presence of the Lord when he sang. And Mom Pearl... She hugged him so hard he thought he would suffocate. "You sing even better than your Daddy," she told him. Miss Pat rushed up to Nate and said, "Child, when you gonna sing again cause I'll surely be there."

Mrs. Miller pulled her car up to Mama's house. She reached over and touched the back of Nate's hand. "I couldn't be more proud of you if you were my own son," she said. As he walked up to his door, Nate felt proud, more proud of himself than he had ever felt before. Maybe he wasn't cursed. Maybe he would realize his dreams. He couldn't wait to share his glorious day with Mama. He burst through the screen door.

Mama was fixing her hair in the cracked mirror that hung over the washbasin. "Mama, I'm home," he called.

"There you be. Where the hell have you been?"

"At church, Mama. Don't you remember? I had my first concert today."

"Oh. Yeah, yeah."

"Mama, it was great. I sang..."

Mama wasn't paying attention. She continued to fuss with her hair. "Child, I don't have time for that. Aint you got to sweep the house?"

"Mama, I did it before I left."

"Well, go sweep the porch off. I needs to have this place lookin' spic and span."

"Yes, ma'am."

As a crestfallen Nate turned to get the broom, Mama came up behind him, grabbed him by the shoulders and spun him around. "He's comin' home today, child. CW's comin' home today." Mama looked so excited. She took Nate's hand in hers and danced him around and around in a circle. This rare show of exuberance left Nate speechless. "My man's comin' home today," Mama crooned as she let go of his hands and Nate careened into a chair. Mama laughed and laughed. "Now go on, sweep that porch. I got to make myself pretty."

James sat on the end of the porch chewing on a piece of dried grass as Nate swept around him. "My Daddy's comin' home," he said with no trace of his mother's enthusiasm. James never understood why his Daddy left him in the first place, and he couldn't comprehend his sudden return. He kind of liked having Mama all to himself, and he certainly didn't miss his father's sharper discipline. He could always win over his Mama; with his father it wasn't quite as easy.

Nate swept and worried about what was to come. Carl Lee had been at Mama's house just two nights ago. He wondered what CW would do if he knew.

A few hours later, an old yellow cab pulled up. CW jumped out looking sharp in his army private's uniform. Mama rushed out the door and jumped into his arms. The two embraced for a long time. Mama cried with joy. "Where's my boy?" CW asked. He turned and saw James peeking out from behind the edge of the porch. "Well come here and give your Daddy a big ol' hug."

James approached him sheepishly. CW picked up and lifted him into the air. "You sure have grown," he said. "You're practically a man!"

James laughed. "Nah, I'm not," he said.

Nate watched the family reunion from the stoop. They were all smiles and happy. "Let me get my bags out the trunk," said CW.

"Nate, get on over here and help your father," Mama said.

Nate raced over to the car and picked up two heavy duffle bags. By the time he turned around, the family was already inside. CW never even acknowledged Nate's presence.

Mama went all out that evening and cooked a big dinner of fried chicken and corn bread. Nate ate his fill while the others laughed and talked for hours. CW regaled his wife and son with tales of his time in the army. He told of the mean drill sergeant who made his platoon march for hours in the rain when two of the privates got into a fight. James's jaw dropped when his Daddy told him running for three miles straight in the hot sun was an every day occurrence. Nate sat silently and listened, wishing he could sneak down to the lake and drink a bottle of Orange Driver he had hidden there. But there would be no chance for that. Mama sent Nate and James to bed early that night. In the middle of the night Nate awoke to the sound of Mama's muffled giggles. He put his pillow over his head and tried to go back to sleep, but he couldn't. In the pit of his stomach there was a gnawing feeling, like something bad was about to happen. After what seemed like an eternity, he drifted off.

The next morning Mama's face was practically glowing. She and CW sat across the table and stared into each other's eyes. It was like they had never been apart. Mama felt calm and peaceful. CW had been right. The separation as difficult as it had been for her had been good for them. She secretly hoped she had gotten pregnant last night. Another baby would be just the thing to make their marriage strong and healthy again. CW wasn't so sure about his marriage, but it did feel so good to be home after his harsh life in the army. Even the shotgun shack on the plantation was more comfortable than barracks living. He was so happy to see James. He wondered if there was a chance they could be a family again. After all, he had changed. The army had matured him. He felt more ready to settle down.

Mama had to go to Miss Ann's to milk the cows that morning and CW decided to go down to the store and see some of his old friends. "Hurry back," Mama told him. "I shouldn't be too long." CW blew her a kiss as he left. Nate watched as Mama giggled. He went over and hugged her around the waist.

It was getting dark by the time CW returned home. He stumbled in the door drunk. "Woman, get your ass over here," he called angrily. Nate was washing out his school clothes in a basin on the porch as CW approached.

Mama rushed up to her husband. "Baby, what's the matter." A wave of fear rushed over her. In an instant she realized he knew her secret.

Almost instinctively, Nate came inside to watch over his Mama.

"What's this I hear about you and Carl Lee?" CW demanded.

Mama reached out and tried to take her husband's hands, but he pulled away. She knew he'd find out, but she didn't imagine it would be this soon. "Well, you was gone," was all she could manage to say.

CW slapped his hand onto his forehead. "And you couldn't wait. I told you I'd be back. I told you we needed time. Damn." He walked over and stood in front of the screen door his back to Mama.

Mama went over to him and stroked his hair. "Baby, it don't mean nothin', I swear. I love you. Now that you're back everything's gonna be different. We're a family again. We'll be happy. I promise. I'll never see him again."

CW turned around and looked Mama straight in the eyes. "How could you? Why did you do this to me?"

Mama sat down on the floor. She pulled up the hem of her blouse and dried her eyes. "Baby, I swear I don't know. I was so lonely and tired, taking care of Miss Ann, and the cotton, and my boys. My Mama told me to go find me a man. She say I shouldn't be alone all the time."

CW laughed out loud. "Your Mama?" He slammed a fist down on the table. "Your Mama?" he shouted.

Mama was startled. She got up and went toward her husband, sobbing, almost hysterical. "Baby, I'm sorry. I'm so sorry. Please forgive me." She reached out to him.

CW pushed her hand away. "Get off me," he said. He looked at her with such contempt that Nate feared he would hit her.

"Your Mama controls you, but she aint gonna control me. I'm leavin."

With that CW went into the sleeping room closed up his barely unpacked duffle bags and stormed out the door. Mama collapsed onto the floor, sobbing uncontrollably. Nate tried to comfort her, but she was inconsolable.

CW never came back.

Mama would soon find out that Carl Lee had enough of her, too. When he found out that CW had returned, Carl Lee started seeing another woman and soon married her. Mama was alone again.

Nate's heart ached for her. Every Sunday, he sang his heart out in church, and every Sunday he tried to make a deal with God. Closing his eyes tightly as the preacher stood in front the congregation arms spread out in benediction, Nate prayed as hard as he could, "Lord, please take care of my Mama. Please make my Mama happy."

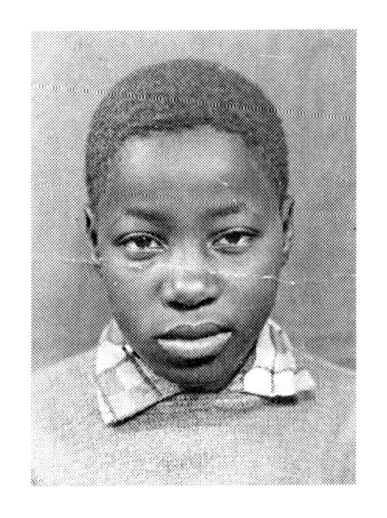

Nate Lowe in 1954 at age eight

The Lowe family shack on the plantation where Nate was born and where he lived from 1946 to 1950 and from 1961 to 1966

The five-acre plot of cotton the Lowe family worked for Mr. Charlie, looking toward the center of the plantation and the road that comes up from the lake

Mr. Charlie's plantation store

The cotton gin in Lake Washington, Mississippi

House used by Nate's Aunt Lubae and Uncle Mark. Aunt Lubae was Ma Pearl's daughter.

Pleasant Star Church in Chatham, Mississippi

The house on the right was Big Mama's sister Aunt Sarah's house on Tallahatchie Street in Clarksdale, Mississippi

Nate in his graduation picture from O'Bannon High School in 1966. Because Negro children were kept from school to work the fields in his early years, Nate was twenty years old when he graduated.

Nate pictured when he graduated from Coahoma College. Nate remembers he wore the same shirt to meet Dr. King, who was assassinated only a few days later.

Nate and Mathilda Griffin in 1969 in front of his Dodge Super B. Nate was on his way to pick up Mama to bring her to St. Louis.

Mathilda Griffin, whom Nate called his "play mother," and who was his inspiration and a stabilizing force in his life

Chapter Twelve

One afternoon in March of 1959, Nate returned from working in the field and got the biggest surprise of his life. Mama called to him from the kitchen. "Nathaniel, Nathaniel, come quick and see who's here!"

Nate hurried through the sitting room and back into the kitchen. He had never heard his Mama sound so happy and excited. He could hardly wait to see who it was. Mama stood with her arms wrapped around a teenaged black boy. He was a few inches taller than Nate. The spitting image of Teenie. The boy chaffed a bit at Mama's embrace. He looked as though he wished he were somewhere else. Nate stood staring not knowing who this kid was.

"Look, child, it's your brother, Manual," Mama crooned. "Don't ya know him?"

The two boys didn't move. Nate barely remembered his brother at all, and he certainly didn't recognize this person who had grown into a young man in the years away from home. It appeared that Manual didn't recognize him either, or Mama for that matter. He stood awkwardly being hugged by a woman his Daddy had told him was his Mama, but who was a stranger to him.

"Well, go on then," Mama said to Nate, "Give your brother a hug."

Nate approached Manual and the two engaged in a weak embrace. Manual smiled at Nate. "Hey, brother, how's it goin', man." He reached out and patted Nate on the shoulder, seeing in his younger brother a potential ally.

Manual's father had raised him for seven years in Chicago, but lately Manual had become a problem. He acted out at school, had some minor run ins with the law, and had been sent to reform school. Emanual Sr. just didn't want to deal with his son anymore, so he sent him back to live with his mother. Mama was so happy to be reunited with her child. She never thought of the difficulties her son would bring into her life.

Mama was ecstatic. For weeks after Manual's arrival, she was overjoyed to have her long, lost son back. She didn't even think about her CW. Even Big Mama's railing about Mama's failures did not get her down. Nate was pleased to see his Mama feeling so good. He wished it would last forever.

Manual, true to his heritage, was worthless in the cotton field. He tried at first, but one day that all ended. Mama, Nate and Manual were picking cotton on a hot summer's late afternoon when they saw Mr. Charlie's car driving up the road in his shiny new Ford. "Look sharp, boys," Mama whispered to her sons, "Mr. Charlie's comin'."

The car stopped next to the last row of cotton plants. The stalks were full of bolls nearly bursting out in fluffy white. Nate was annoyed by Mr. Charlie's intrusion. He had work to do to make the quota and precious little daylight left.

Mr. Charlie, followed by his son Elm, walked up between the rows. The three cotton pickers stopped and turned to face him. "What the hell are you niggers gawking at?" Mr. Charlie shouted in his shrill nasal voice. "Get back to work. Look at these plants. This cotton's gotta be picked before it rots."

Mama and Nate returned to picking, but Manual didn't appreciate Mr. Charlie's tone. He stood and stared somewhat defiantly.

Mr. Charlie walked straight up to Manual and stopped inches from the boy's face. "What you lookin' at, nigger?"

Mama, who was standing next to Manual, took hold of his arm and tugged at his sleeve in a silent plea for him to back down. Manual was not stupid. He knew the ways of the world when it came to black and white. Cautiously he turned around and reached for a ripe cotton boll. Just as he was about to pull the boll off the plant, Mr. Charlie pushed him, hurling him to the ground. Mama ran to her son. She held him down on the ground, stopping his defiant instinct to get up and fight. Mr. Charlie stood over him. "I said, what you lookin' at nigger?"

Nate was panicked. He knew Manual had a streak of hostility in him. In the short time Manual had been back home. Nate had seen him fuss and yell at Mama on more than one occasion. He frustrated easily and when he did, he lashed out. Nate worried that his brother might end up hanging from a tree limb one day. "Mr. Charlie, he don't know. He lived up north," Nate begged. " Please leave him be, sir. We don't want no trouble."

Mr. Charlie turned toward Nate, surprised yet not surprised by his impertinence. Just as he was about to speak, Elm intervened. "Daddy, the boy's right. He's new here. Only just come from Chicago. He don't know." Elm stepped in between his father and Manual. "Come on, Daddy," he said. "Let's get back to the house. It's almost supper time."

Mr. Charlie took out his handkerchief and wiped his brow. He adjusted his hat and turned to walk away with his son. "Damn, niggers," he grumbled. "I swear they'll be the death of me yet."

As his father walked to the car, Elm reached out a hand to Manual and helped him back up to his feet. "Thank you, Mr. Elm," Mama said, " You sure is a blessing to us all."

"You're welcome, Willie B," he said smiling. "Now you best all get back to work."

"Yes, sir, we will sir," Mama replied.

As soon as Mr. Charlie's car pulled away, Manual halted his attempts at cotton picking. "Man," he shouted, "I'm gonna kick his ass. Where he get off talkin' to me that way? Shit."

Mama dropped her sack and went over to her son. "Manual," she said sternly, "don't you be talkin' that way."

Manual spun around and faced Mama. "Shit, don't tell me how to talk," he said. "I'll talk the way I wanna talk. And I'll kick his ass if I wanna."

Mama reached inside her pants pocket and pulled out her handkerchief. She walked away from her sons sobbing. She feared her newfound son would get himself killed with that mouth of his.

Manual grinned at Nate. "What's her problem?"

Nate could have said something. He could have said a lot, but that was not his way. He returned to picking. Precious time had already been lost.

The picking season was coming to an end, and each day there were fewer and fewer cotton bolls on the stalks. Nate finished picking early in the afternoon and was starting to walk to Big Mama's house. She had gone to Glen Allan, so he thought he'd spend the afternoon with Paw Paw drinking some of his grandfather's corn whiskey. Nate didn't like the way the corn whiskey tasted but he liked how it made him feel. He only had to drink a little to feel really good.

As he made his way across Mr. Charlie's plantation, Nate worried about the approaching settlement. Even with the meager help of Manual the family was again unlikely to make enough to impress Mr. Charlie and receive a settlement. Even if they had made their quota Nate knew the family would owe, according to Mr. Charlie, and his opinion was all that mattered. Nate was sure Mr. Charlie had it in for his family. He didn't' know why.

All of a sudden, Nate heard the thumping of horse's hooves. He turned to see Mr. Elm riding up to him.

"Afternoon," Elm said.

"Afternoon, sir."

"I need a couple men to help me round up the cows. Meet me down at the pasture."

"Yes, sir." There went his afternoon of relaxation.

When he reached the cow pasture Carl Lee. West Neuman, Horseman, Jimmy Lee and some other men were already there. "Damn," said Carl Lee as Nate walked up, "I hope this don't take long. I gots work to do before the sun goes down."

"Yup, so do I," said Jimmy Lee.

Carl Lee looked at Nate. "How's your Mama doin'?" he asked sheepishly. "I hope she's fine. I never wish any bad on her, you know."

"She doin' fine." Nate said. Carl Lee was a decent enough guy. He just got caught up in a mess.

"No hard feelings?" Carl Lee asked.

"None," said Nate.

After a few minutes passed, Elm rode up to the men. "I want you boys to stand by the gate and when I get the herd inside pull the gate shut behind."

"Yes, sir, Mr. Elm," Nate called to him as he rode away to the backside of the pasture where the cows had gathered. It was time to round them up for their initial branding. The rest of the men, six or so, waited on the other side of the corral ready to jump in and help with the branding.

Jimmy Lee, Carl Lee and Nate stood by the open gate of the corral and watched Elm as he reached the herd. He started to circle around back of them to get them moving toward the men. Suddenly, something spooked Elm's chestnut stallion. The horse reared up once and then again. The third time the panicked horse reared Elm fell off and the top of his head hit the ground.

Nate ran to help Mr. Charlie's son. The stallion had run off, but Elm lay still on the brown pasture grass. Blood ran out from the corner of his mouth. His eyes were fixed to the sky as if he were staring at something indescribably beautiful. "Mr. Elm, are you all right?" Nate asked frantically. "Mr. Elm, can you hear me?"

Carl Lee and Jimmy Lee stumbled up behind Nate, panting and gasping for air. Carl Lee took one look at Elm and said, "Lord almighty, he look like he dead."

Fear shot through Nate's body. He couldn't be dead. He just couldn't be. Nate walked around to the other side of Elm's body and saw a sight that took his breath. The side of Elm's skull was crushed. It looked like pieces of his brain lay in the dirt. "Run, go get Mr. Charlie," he screamed.

Carl Lee and Jimmy Lee didn't move. Carl Lee's eyes were big as silver dollars.

"Run, I said."

Jimmy Lee stammered, "What I supposed to tell him?"

"I don't know…." Nate wanted to grab his ignorant cohort by the shoulders and shake him good and hard. "Just get him," Nate yelled so loud the entire herd ran to the other side of the pasture.

Jimmy Lee ran straight for the big house fast as he could run.

Nate knelt down next to Elm and grabbed hold of his hand. He recited a prayer Mom Pearl had taught him and begged God to save this man who was the sharecroppers' only friend and ally. Softly, he began to sing a hymn. Elm's hand was growing cold.

All of a sudden Nate was physically thrust aside. Mr. Charlie pressed a bony finger to the side of his son's neck. The old man pulled back, let out a terrible shriek, and collapsed on his son's chest. Nate, Carl Lee, and Jimmy Lee stood to one side. Mr. Charlie's wife ran up, but her husband jumped up and held her back. "He's gone," Mr. Charlie sobbed. "Our boy is gone." Miss Ann collapsed in her husband's arms.

For the next few days, the sheriff's came and investigated Elm's death. Mr. Charlie swore it was the niggers that did it. They were disobeying. They spooked the horse. Someone had to be blamed.

The sharecroppers were justly afraid, especially the families of the workmen who had been there that fateful day. Mama cried and cried afraid her son would be the one to take the fall.

Nate wasn't afraid, though. He knew what had happened. Of all the people on the plantation Elm was about the last one he wanted to see dead. As Elm lay on the dirt, Nate wished only that he could be saved.

The sheriff sat Mr. Charlie down the day after the funeral and told Mr. Charlie it looked like it was an accident, a horrible accident. "I investigated the scene and talked to all the colored that was there," he told him. "Everything checks out." Mr. Charlie stared at the sheriff and then dropped his head down covering his face with his hands.

After a few weeks, the incident was not spoken of again.

Miraculously, the powers that be had sided with the sharecroppers. Miss Pat told the old women of the plantation, "In all my days, that aint never happened before and sure as I'm standin' it aint likely to happen again."

Chapter Thirteen

It had rained that day and by the time Mr. Sylvester and Nate had walked to Pleasant Star both were soaked. Miss Minnie Barksdale took Nate into the choir room behind the altar and helped him dry off with some old cloth she found under the money-counting table. "Child, you is wet down to the bone," she said, laughing as she fluffed his hair dry.

Nate had a hangover from a long evening of commiserating with a bottle of Morgan Davis on Saturday night. He knew he shouldn't have drunk so much, but he couldn't help himself. A pain had risen up inside of him. The old hatred for Mr. Charlie roared him like a hungry lion. The incident a few days before with Manual only whetted the lion's appetite. The hunger turned on him and he feared it would eat him alive. After a few sips of the grape flavored elixer, the roaring subsided, and soon went away completely.

"There now," Miss Minnie said as she dried the back of Nate's new brown suit, "you lookin' presentable enough to sing."

Nate thought to himself, "I might look presentable, but I sure don't feel that way." He smiled broadly at Miss Minnie. "Thank you, ma'am," he said sheepishly, not used to such coddling.

"Oh, it aint nuthin'. You gots to look good to stand in front of the whole church. Now go on, get on out there."

Nate went out and took his place with the choir behind the pulpit. Everyone was already seated. The church was full to capacity, in spite of the inclement weather. They were there to hear their most prized brother sing. Mom Pearl, Aunt Loobay, and Aunt Dago smiled and waved at him from the front row. Mom Pearl beamed with pride. She never missed one of her grandson's performances. Miss Minnie took her place at the old piano. She caught Nate's eye and smiled at him, feeling the same anticipation she did each time her protégé sang.

Nate straightened the lapels of his new suit. It was a sort of parting gift from Mrs. Miller. She had explained to him that she could no longer be his pianist and take him to his singing engagements. As much as she loved accompanying him, the demands of work and family were becoming too great. Nate understood. "Now you remember I'll always be here to help if you need advice or just an ear to listen," she told him. "And who knows, if you're in a pinch I'll fill in at the piano. All you have to do is ask."

There was no shortage of volunteers to accompany Nate on the piano at his singing engagements, so popular and admired was he. Nate settled on two ladies who had been most encouraging to him since the beginning: Miss Minnie Barksdale and Miss Mathilda Griffin, whom Nate called his play mother. They graciously and enthusiastically made sure that one of them played for him wherever he traveled to sing.

The service began and soon it was Nate's turn. He arose from his seat and sang with the choir. He felt his hangover melt away, and a feeling of joy reverberated in his heart. When his solo arrived, the music flowed out from deep inside him. It flowed through him and out to the congregation in a whoosh of sound as though he didn't control it, as though it didn't come from him.

After the service, Miss Mathilda Griffin jumped up from the piano and pushed through the crowd, grabbed Nate by the shoulders and took him off to the side. Her expression was strong and determined as though nothing could stop her. The force with which she took his hand took Nate aback. "Child, the Lord has spoken to me this day, she said with conviction. "He has told me to look out for you and your talent."

Nate was a bit bewildered. "Yes, ma'am?"

Miss Mathilda raised her hands up to the ceiling. "The Lord has spoken to me," she said. She leaned back her head and cast her eyes up to the ceiling of the church. "He has told me that I must see that you get off the plantation. He has told me He has greater plans for you, yes, sir, this He has told me, and this I will do for Him. Don't you worry."

By this time a small crowd of people had gathered around Nate and Miss Mathilda. "Praise the Lord," exclaimed Miss Minnie Barksdale.

"Praise the Lord," the crowd echoed.

Nate smiled. Her words were most amazing. She believed in him and so did the Lord and He would help. He would help. It was a miracle. There at the back of the crowd stood Mom Pearl smiling with pride at her grandson.

A few days later Nate was working in the cotton field. A cloud of dust billowed in the distance; rising high over the cotton plants winding it's way toward where Nate and a few other sharecroppers were working. Miss Pat rushed over and grabbed Nate's wrist. "Mr. Charlie's comin'."

Nate paused briefly, and then returned to his work. Plenty of cotton to be picked. A quota to be met. This year would be the first time his family got a settlement. Nate just knew it. If the Lord was helping him with his singing, surely, He would help his family, too. Surely. If only Nate worked hard as he could. He began to sing to recapture his picking rhythm. His nimble fingers twisted and tugged the plump white bolls off the branches and quickly deposited them into his sack. "My baby don't need to worry no more, she don't need to beg and steal…"

Suddenly he felt a poke in the middle of his back. He wheeled around to see Mr. Charlie extending the handle of a hoe toward him. Nate turned back around without saying anything, annoyed at the interruption in his work.

"Boy, you turn your ass around and face me," Mr. Charlie boomed. Nate obeyed. "That's better." Mr. Charlie's older son Bo snickered and took the hoe from his father. Bo had left the plantation and joined the military, hoping to make a life of his own somewhere else. After Elm was killed, he was forced to return and help his father. One day Bo would be in charge. It was his duty.

Bo had no sympathy for the niggers that worked for his father and none of the compassion of his older brother. Things had certainly changed since Elm's death. Miss Ann barely showed her face, taking to her bed for months after the death of her son. Mama worked twice as hard to keep Mr. Charlie's house going. She even labored on the weekends to keep the big house's flower gardens from dying for lack of Miss Ann's patient attention.

Mr. Charlie's face aged overnight. Lines and creases appeared and deepened. His gait became slower and labored. In spite of this he visited the fields more often. Last week he shoved Carl Lee and pushed him to the ground. A few days ago he screamed at Miss Pat and brought her to tears. Nate didn't think it was possible, but since Elm's death, Mr. Charlie had gotten even meaner than before.

Nate lowered his gaze toward the ground, unwilling to look Mr. Charlie in the eyes. "Bo, lookie here, look at this crazy boy," Mr. Charlie said.

Bo laughed out loud. "I see him, Daddy."

Nate winced. In his mind he saw Mr. Charlie with horns and a tail, carrying a pitchfork—the devil in the flesh and standing right in front of him.

"Look at me, nigger. I got somethin' to ask you," Mr. Charlie said in his stale Southern drawl. "That's better."

Nate looked at him, but looked through him, almost as if he wasn't there.

"I hear you're goin' to school. What the hell do you want to do that for?" Mr. Charlie's words were followed by the chuckles of his son.

"I'm goin' to school to get an education."

Now Mr. Charlie laughed out loud. "Boy, you don't need an education to hoe my cotton."

Nate looked the devil straight in the eyes, stared long and hard and said, "I don't plan to hoe cotton for the rest of my life."

Mr. Charlie guffawed and slapped the side of his leg. He turned to Bo and said, "Did you hear that, son? Did you ever hear anything so ridiculous?"

"No, Daddy, I don't think I ever did." Bo wiped sweat from his forehead with a red bandana and pushed up the brim of his gray straw hat.

Nate's eyes remained focused on Mr. Charlie's, and the bossman abruptly stopped laughing. This boy was strange, crazy, different. The old man felt a pang of fear. The boy was way too uppity. He needed to be kept in line. Knowledge could cause him to forget his place in the scheme of things. Knowledge could make him lash out. This was not good; this was not good at all. A dumb nigger trying to be smart—that could only spell trouble.

Without saying another word, Mr. Charlie turned and left. Bo stood in his spot for a moment, surprised by his father's quick retreat, but he soon followed. After that day, Mr. Charlie treated Nate differently than he had before, avoiding him as much as possible. Nate represented what he most deeply feared—the change that would destroy his way of life.

On their first day of high school, Nate and Chip stood in front of O'Bannon High feeling very small. The old red brick school looked so big to them. Nate was anxious. He had felt so at home at Chatham Elementary and Moore Middle School, both schools had a kind of neighborhood feel. O'Bannon was much larger, and twenty-five miles from the Mr. Charlie's plantation. It was operated by the Westernline School District in Washington County, which supervised elementary, junior high and high school students throughout Washington County, Mississippi

Lionel took a deep breath. "Come on, Lowe. Let's go on in."

Nate followed somewhat reluctantly, crunching through the dead leaves from the large weeping willow tree that graced the front courtyard. The fragrance of the sweet crushed leaves permeated the air. As he looked around the beauty of his new school amazed Nate. There was a real gymnasium and a cafeteria. The classrooms were large and spacious made to hold thirty or more students; the desks were made of thick heavy oak wood and had actual drawers in them. He would soon learn that once again everything here was a cast off. The books were once used by the white students at Greenville High, and there weren't enough of them to go around, so two children had to share each book. When it came time to study for a test, one child took the book home one night and the other book sharer took it home the next. Even the Confederate flag that flew over the school was left over from the former whites-only school.

The boys found their way into their classroom and took seats next to each other. They saw a few kids they knew from Moore, but most of the ninth graders came from other junior highs in the area. Mrs. Smith, Miss Huston, Miss Jackson, and Mr. Chambers stood in front of the class and told them what to expect at O'Bannon. They would have to buy and bring their own paper and pencils. Chalk was at a premium and was handed out to teachers at the beginning of each week and was to be used sparingly.

Mrs. Williams came into the room after the administrators had left. Handing out textbooks, she was explained that she was their English teacher with a lot of learning to offer them. She instructed them to read a selection from the works of Walt Whitman for homework that evening. Lionel looked over at Nate and smiled. Walt Whitman was one of Lionel's favorite authors.

A knock came at the wooden classroom door. A distinguished looking bald man with a white goatee entered the room. He wore a crisp blue suit, white shirt and tie, and Stacy Adams shoes. Miss Williams introduced him as Mr. Williams, the principal. He addressed the class speaking slowly in a strong voice. He told the class of the many opportunities at O'Bannon, the importance of their studies, and at the end he got in a plug for the school's sports programs, encouraging the students to take part in athletics.

Nate listened intently to Mr. Williams, as he always did when a teacher was speaking. It was obvious that Mr. Williams was a very wise and intelligent man. Instinctively, Nate knew it was important to pay the closest attention to every word this man said. For a boy who so badly wanted to learn how to live his own life, an intelligent, successful black man was a better resource than the largest library in Mississippi.

After Mr. Williams left, Mrs. Williams returned to her lesson. English was always the most difficult subject for Nate, who learned to read and write later in his life than most children. And Mrs. Williams, he could tell, was going to be tough. He groaned inside as he thought of dealing with her throughout his high school years. As he struggled to read his Walt Whitman assignment, he envisioned many a red "F" written across the tops of his papers.

Chip leaned over, as if he were reading Nate's mind and said, "Don't worry. I'll help you."

Nate looked at his friend and smiled. Chip was true to his word, and Nate's mind was instantly eased. If he had never realized what a blessing his friend was, he understood in that moment.

The rest of the day flew by except for the lunch period. Nate sneaked outside and hung around until lunch ended. He didn't have money to buy his food and there was no food at home to bring for lunch. By this time, Chip knew to go to lunch alone and not to offer to pay or try to coax Nate to go to the cafeteria. It was best to leave his friend be.

In the afternoon, Nate met Mr. Carter the shop teacher. Mr. Carter talked about crafting with wood like it was a religious experience. Nate could not wait to get started. His mind was swimming with projects he'd like to attempt. Later, as he rode home on the rickety school bus, Nate mused about Mr. Carter's ability to motivate people. He wanted to be like him. Someday he wanted to work at inspiring people like his teacher did. Nate didn't know how he would do it, but deep down he knew he would one day. One day Nate Lowe would be somebody, too.

Chapter Fourteen

Around the age of fourteen, Nate became very focused on his personal grooming. He always wanted to look his best. Being a plantation celebrity because of his singing, he had to look good at all times, especially on Sunday mornings when he stood up in front of a standing room only congregation. Many things about his appearance he could not control—most notably his wardrobe. Money for fine, stylish suits, silk ties, and snappy wing tip shoes was simply not in the picture. Mrs. Miller had ever so kindly given him some clothes that made him look quite presentable. The outfits she gave him saved him the embarrassment and humiliation over his attire that had plagued him throughout most of his life.

A determined young man like Nate could control and improve upon many things about his personal presentation, and he set about making those improvements with the zeal that made him a standout among cotton pickers. He discovered that rubbing just a touch of lard onto his hands before bed softened the cracked, brittle skin work in the cotton fields created. He found that if he wet a rag and soaped it up thoroughly, he could wash up his face and body in one motion and rinse by wetting the rag only two or three times. In this way he could bathe every evening using a minimum of precious water. If he rinsed out the rag very well, he could use it to scrub his teeth, too.

But the one thing that troubled him was his hair. He liked to keep it nice and neat, short and close to his head. To his dismay, it seemed it grew faster than the little ragweed plants that sprung up overnight all along the cotton rows. No sooner had he gotten his haircut, it became too long and unruly again. He didn't like paying the twenty-five cents each time, and the men on the plantation who cut hair didn't much like doing it. As a result, their work was frequently below Nate's high standard. Frustrated, Nate decided to teach himself to cut his own hair. He'd save money and could keep his hair looking good all the time.

Making sure that no one saw him, especially James and Manual, Nate went behind Mama's house to the place where he had buried the coins he had saved. He carefully dug up the old Prince Albert tobacco can. He pulled the rusted, beat up, old tin out of the dry brown earth and pried off the lid. Taking money from his savings was not something he did lightly, but this was important. He took four dollars in quarters from the can and quickly shoved them into the pocket of his dirty blue jeans. "If hair clippers cost more than a four dollars, then I just aint getting 'em," he told himself. He returned the can to the hole, covered it with dirt, and packed it down. He replaced the weeds and twigs he used to camouflage his secret.

At Roy Shank's store on Lake Washington, he proudly bought a pair of clippers for three dollars and seventy-five cents. Little did he know his barbering days were only just beginning.

He quickly found that trying to learn on his own head was a difficult task. It became apparent that he needed to learn and practice on some human guinea pigs. He approached Mama's friend Horseman, offering to cut his hair for free. Horseman eagerly agreed and sat down on the porch stoop to let Nate work. Nate produced his shiny new clippers. Just as he was about to begin, Horseman began to have misgivings. "Now Poonie, you know what you doin', right?" he asked. Most of Mama's friends and family called Nate by the nickname Poonie.

"Sure I do," Nate said confidently, hoping he could follow through with his claim.

Horseman turned around to face him, carefully surveying Nate's face for falsehood. "All right, then Poonie, go on. Just don't make me look like no porcupine or nuthin'." He smiled good-naturedly opening up his large, thick lips and showing his teeth yellowed by heavy cigarette smoking.

Nate began to cut tentatively, but then became more deliberate. He found that if he took off only a little at a time he could always go back and fix uneven spots. Soon he realized cutting hair was not so difficult as he had imagined.

Horseman seemed to relax as Nate cut. He seemed to sense that Nate was being cautious and wanted to do a good job. After a while, he started talking to fill the silence. "You know, Poonie," he said, "my wife's all right, but I gots to find me a part-time lover."

Nate winced. Horseman talked about that subject all the time almost incessantly.

"I gots to get me some side action," he continued. "I can't have just one woman the rest of my life. You know what I mean?"

"Uh huh," Nate said to appease him. He started to cut a little faster, so he wouldn't have to hear much more of Horseman's ramblings.

When he finished, Nate had to admit ol' Horseman was looking very good. He took out a red plastic encased hand mirror and handed it to his guinea pig. Horseman looked and patted and fluffed. "Damn, boy, you done good. Real good. Thank you kindly."

Nate smiled back at him. He had done a good job and was proud of himself. Little did he know what his little experiment would start and what it would mean to him and his future

With Horseman's freshly trimmed mane as his advertisement, Nate's reputation as a barber took root. Soon all sorts of plantation men were coming to him and asking for his services. Nate was happy to comply and practice. He was in training—training to cut his own hair to perfection. Before he was through he had to invest a few cents in some more pocket mirrors, devising a system of setting then up on the porch so that he could see his head from all angles. Soon he had accomplished his goal. His hair was looking neatly coiffed all the time.

He no longer needed to work on volunteers having mastered his craft. But the men of the plantation were hooked on his work. They would not stop asking him to cut their hair. Finally, Nate gave in, but told them it would now cost them twenty-five cents, and he'd only cut hair on Saturday afternoon. Soon the line of customers stretched clear over to the woodpile at the back of Mama's house. At twenty-five cents a pop, Nate was making quite a side income for himself. Every Saturday night, he'd take out a dollar for a bottle of Orange Driver and the rest would be deposited into the old Prince Albert can. After a few weeks, he needed to add a second can and then a third…

At school Nate met the football coach Mr. Redmond, who encouraged him to go out for the team. Nate was impressed by Coach. He was a tall man, dressed casually wearing a jacket with the school emblem on it. He was light skinned and wore black plastic Buddy Holly glassed with thick lenses and bifocals. He was kind, but firm and no nonsense, the type of man who knew how to get the job done. Nate liked that. Soon Nate was proudly wearing the O'Bannon High School red, green and white football uniform.

Each morning before practice, Mr. Redmond addressed his players. He stressed the importance of a good education above all else even sport. Without fail, he kept tabs on his players' academic performance, and all his boys knew it. If he saw one of his players loitering in the halls while classes were in session, he'd take him by the arm and get him to the class where he belonged.

One crisp November evening Mr. Redmond stood before his players on the choppy playing field behind the high school. That day he was dressed in a fine blue suit with a gray tie, looking very proud and handsome in his business attire. "Before we start practice today, men, I want to talk to you about your futures," he said in his heavy low pitched voice.

A few of the players around Nate groaned quietly. They didn't want a lecture; they wanted to slam and block and pass. They got enough of being talked to in class. Nate looked at one of them disdainfully. Coach was talking. Everyone should listen up and listen up good.

"In Mississippi the black man is controlled by the white man. Why? Because many black men are ignorant."

Nate took off his helmet so he could hear coach better, instinctively knowing he wanted to soak up every word.

"You men have to finish school and go on to college. With an education the white man can't control you. It's the only way you can truly be your own man."

Nate and Chip already knew how important an education was

to their futures. They both planned to go to college, although Nate had no idea how he would do it. Mama needed him to work the fields, but most of all he had no idea how he could ever afford the tuition. Still he remained determined to go.

"Listen up all of you. No one can control you if you've got a good education. Hear that if you hear nothing else I say. It's the most important thing I will ever tell you," Mr. Redmond said, pacing back and forth in front of the ragtag line of players. His voice was strong and quivered with emotion as he finished his speech. "Now go on get out there and do five laps around the field."

The other players eagerly started running, relieved that the lecture had ended. But Nate's mind was abuzz. That was it. Control. Mr. Charlie controlled him. Mr. Charlie controlled his Mama. Honestly, he hated Mr. Charlie for many reasons, but it was that control over him and his Mama that he resented the most. And here was the key. Nate vowed he'd find a way to go to college. It was the only hope for him and for his Mama.

One of the other players lost his footing and bumped Nate's side. The player almost collapsed in laughter. "Watch out, you clumsy ox," he joked. Nate kept on running. He looked back sternly at the jokester. No time for fooling around. Nate was serious, dead serious.

And that set the tone for the next several years of Nate's life. He worked hard at school and on the football field. He went out for baseball and track and did his best at each. His prowess in athletics and good looks made him the object of many a crush for his female classmates, but Nate had no time for any of them. More important goals consumed him.

Still, getting to school was a struggle. Mama needed his picking talent to make the quota. Mr. Redmond grew very concerned over Nate's missed days, as had Nate's teachers in the past. When he found Nate absent, he would drive out to the plantation and bring Nate to school for evening practice. After practice, he'd sit Nate down and encourage him to be more diligent in his school attendance. Mr. Redmond never pushed too hard, knowing full and well the pressures Nate faced. Nate appreciated that, and he also valued Mr. Redmond's gentle encouragement.

The football team had played its first four games and won every one. They were doing better than Nate had anticipated. As he rode the rickety school bus to class on a dark, cold morning in late November, Nate passed the time going over plays in his head. The elementary school kids that rode the bus were rowdy that day. Nate could barely concentrate. One of the youngsters, a small, seven year old named Jack jumped up and down on his seat. The bus driver turned full around and told him to settle down, but Jack was too charged up to listen. Another boy at the front of the bus was taunting him. "Shut up, stupid," Jack yelled.

"Come up here and say that Jack McCoy," the boy shouted back.

Jack got up from his seat and in the darkness started to run up to smack the other boy. He took one step, then two, and disappeared through a rusted out hole in the floor of the bus. The bus fell silent for a moment. The other children were shocked by what they had just witnessed. It couldn't be. Yet Jack was gone. "Mr. Kidlans, Mr. Kidlans, you done lost little Jack. He done fell through the floor," cried one of the older boys.

Mr. Kidlans glanced up in his rear view mirror. "What you say?"

"Jack is gone."

One of the girls screamed. Nate stood up in his seat, not knowing what to do. Mr. Kidlans pulled over and walked to the back of the bus. He saw that hole in the floor. It was bigger than it had been when he cleaned out his bus that morning before picking up his charges. "Oh God almighty," he said in disbelief. He ran up to the driver's seat and turned the bus around. He drove back to find Jack, and sure enough a few hundred yards up the road, he saw Jack's crumbled body lying in the middle of the northbound lane. The little boy was dead.

He picked him up and brought him onto the bus, not knowing what else to do. The younger children were sobbing. Mr. Kidlans did his best to calm them on the drive to the school, but he could barely calm himself. Nate sat back in his seat and stared out the window. Blacks always got second best or worse. It was the white man's way of controlling them. And now a little boy was dead. Hot tears welled up in his eyes, but he blinked them back sharply.

That afternoon on the football field his team played its fifth game of the season. Nate blocked hard and ran fast and determined. He had never played better, and his team won again.

Chapter Fifteen

Nate could not stop thinking about little Jack. That night he awoke in the middle of the night. He tossed and turned on the stir mattress. Manual, sleeping next to him, woke up and cursed his brother. "You crazy bastard, knock it off," he whispered angrily. "I need to get some sleep."

Rolling over and shifting away from his brother, Nate winced. Manual hadn't been back on the plantation all that long, but he already heard the gossip about Nate and bought into it. He wondered why Manual needed sleep so badly. Surely it wasn't because he wanted to be fresh for working in the fields and helping his family. More likely he needed his strength to chase women and hang out late at the Green Frog with Teenie.

Shutting his eyes, Nate tried to fall back to sleep, but the old terror rose in his stomach. He felt like he couldn't breathe. It had been a long time since he had one of the night terrors that haunted his early years, but the awful feeling had returned. Now it was even more embarrassing. He was practically a man now, supposed to be strong, not supposed to cry. But, oh, he wanted to cry. He wanted to cry for that little boy, the one that played innocently on the too-dangerous-to-use school bus, the one that laughed and teased his friends, the one that just wanted to live and be happy, but now was dead. Jack reminded Nate so much of himself. An innocent soul that life had dealt so horrible a hand. The accidents of their births had sealed both their fates. In spite of his dreams and aspirations, Nate could not help but feel cursed. Just as little Jack had been.

Looking out the front window, Nate traced a pattern of stars in the clear night sky, trying to quiet his mind. A fresh wave of sadness poured over him. He struggled to suppress his tears, not wanting the humiliation he'd face if Emanual or James heard his sobs. "Maybe little Jack is better off," he thought. "At least the Hell of his life is over." His sadness became despair and threatened to consume him, but suddenly the emotion changed. Unexpressed the feeling staled and hardened. It met the well of anger that lay in his belly always. He began to think of Mr. Charlie, the devil man that controlled his life. He despised his bony face, his haughty walk, the redness of his skin when he was angry, the stale, nasal twang of his voice.

He began to think about killing Mr. Charlie. There were so many ways he could do it, so many opportunities to murder the symbol of his hatred and frustration. Nate didn't even care what would happen to him if he did the deed. He'd be doing God a favor. Yes, he would.

His thoughts of the ultimate revenge strangely calmed him and Nate finally fell back to sleep, feeling much better. There was much work to do.

The next day Nate didn't go to school. The family was horribly behind on their fieldwork. The ground had thawed from a cold spell and needed to be worked so the cotton could be snapped. As always, James and Manual used any excuse not to work in the fields. Mama never wanted to be too hard on her baby James, and now Manual, the prodigal son returned, was receiving similar favored status. Nate, however, was not so lucky. Mama railed at him, told him he was good for nothing and letting his family down. "Don't I take care of you? Don't I work my fingers to the bone for your sorry ass?" she shouted. "And this is how you repay your Mama, by goin' to school and lettin' the fields go to waste."

"Yes, Mama, I know," Nate told her, his stomach sinking as he thought of the lessons and practices he's be missing. Chip would be so disappointed. And coach... He didn't even want to think about it. "Don't you worry, Mama, I'll take care of it. You just go on and go up to Miss Ann's. I won't be goin' to school."

"That's better," Mama said as she tied on her gingham apron. "And don't you go back to school until all the crop is gathered. You aint too old for me to whip your ass good."

"Yes, ma'am."

Mr. Charlie had an old John Deere tractor that he let sharecroppers use on their plots. Nate hoped that no one else was using it so that he could get most of the fieldwork done that day and miss the least amount of class possible. If only he could haul wood today, he could get that done and be back at school on Wednesday. As he approached the tractor yard, there it stood, the old rusty mess that it was. Elated, Nate climbed aboard, started it up, and began to leave the tractor yard on his way to Mama's plot of land.

In his haste to get his work done, Nate had forgotten a critical factor. Mr. Charlie, always concerned that the block on the tractor would freeze up, had his men drain the radiator after each time they used it. Nate had forgotten to fill the radiator with water. As he drove up the dirt road, the old engine sputtered and groaned. Smoke began pouring out of the front, but the momentum of the tractor caused the smoke to billow around the sides and the back where he couldn't see it. Nate drove on, feeling guilty about missing football practice. He imagined the disappointment Mr. Redmond would feel when he saw Nate marked off absent once again. He wondered if Mr. Redmond would make the long trek out to the plantation to talk to Mama again. He dreaded that. It was so embarrassing and Mama would be upset with him for days after.

Suddenly Nate heard a commotion behind him. He could barely make it out over the tractor engine. But soon there it was. Mr. Charlie ran up beside him. He punched the side of the tractor with a bony fist. "What are you doin', nigger," he screamed. "Shut it down. You're ruinin' my engine."

Nate stopped the tractor, and when he did he saw the smoke and realized what he had done.

Mr. Charlie ripped his cigar out of his mouth and threw it down on the dirt. "Get off there, you miserable piece of shit."

Nate looked down at the devil. A cold rage flowed through his body. He felt something clicking in his brain. This was his chance, and he would take it.

Mr. Charlie's face was bright crimson. "Don't you hear me, boy? I said get off my tractor. I oughta beat you within an inch of your life for wreckin' my tractor, you stupid bastard."

Nate picked up the crankshaft and jumped down. He walked over and stood directly in front of Mr. Charlie. Nate's eyes were wide with rage but frozen with determination. He looked right into Mr. Charlie's face and said, "If you bat your eyes, I will kill you."

Mr. Charlie was taken aback, but he stood his ground.

"Tell me if you believe me. If you don't this will be the day you die," Nate said. He had never been more serious. In his right hand he clutched the crankshaft. He gripped it tightly, waiting for a reason to bash in the skull of the demon standing in front of him.

Mr. Charlie started to shake. No one had ever stood up to him like that, especially no nigger. For a moment, he was unable to move, but then he turned around and walked into his store. Once inside, he told his allies. "You better go out and get him. He's gone crazy." Bo came out and talked Nate down. He got him to surrender the crankshaft, and told him to go back to work. As Nate walked out to the field, Bo shook his head. "Damn crazy bastard," he said under his breath. No one ever spoke of the incident again, but Mr. Charlie secretly prayed there would be no further incident with his insane nigger. He hoped Nate would just do his work and not bother anyone. Mr. Charlie surely would not provoke him again. He didn't want to have to do something drastic; Nate was a good cotton picker. But if he had to…

Denied the use of the tractor for that day, Nate picked up a cotton sack and began to pick Mama's acreage of cotton by hand. Mama would be furious, and it would take him the entire week to get the field in shape for planting. He was ashamed of what he had done and afraid. He remembered well the story of Nathaniel, a smart aleck nigger, whom none of the white folks liked much. One day he pushed his bosses too far and in the dead of night they came for him, beat him nearly to death, and threw him in the hog trough where the hogs ate his flesh until he was dead. Nate shuddered as he realized that could happen to him. Or worse. If there were a worse way to die. He had crossed Mr. Charlie in the most blatant way. Surely there would be some kind of reprisal. His hands began to quiver, and he could barely pick the cotton as he straddled the cotton row.

In desperation, Nate considered running away. He could go to

Detroit where a cousin lived. He'd be safe there. He could find a job and make extra money cutting hair to save for college. Life would most likely be better for him there far away from Mr. Charlie's control and reprisals.

Suddenly feeling lightheaded, Nate dropped his sack and sat down in the dirt. All that was just a dream. He could never leave his Mama. Not now. He would just have to stay and hope that Mr. Charlie wouldn't kill him. He raised up onto his knees, bowed his head and began to pray that God would spare his life, that He would put forgiveness into Mr. Charlie's hard heart. Eyes clenched and hands tightly folded, Nate begged God to forgive him, too, for the violence he had nearly committed. He became aware of the sun beating down on his shoulders. His body was warmed and his shaking ceased. He picked up his hoe and began to work again.

One Saturday a few weeks later, Big Mama came by to help Mama dig sweet potatoes in Mama's truck patch behind the shack. She didn't really help though. It was more like supervising with occasional gossip and denigrating comments thrown in for good measure. After he had finished in the fields, Nate came by to help his Mama wash the potatoes. Mama worked so hard growing vegetables and fruits to feed her family all throughout the growing season. He felt very proud of her as he approached and watched her bent over at the waist digging sweet potatoes in the fresh brown earth. The day was lovely and Nate felt good. Even the sight of Big Mama standing, hands on her hips on the garden's edge didn't bother him.

He walked up and put his arm around Mama's waist. She straightened up, looking startled. "Mama, what you want me to do," he asked.

"Lord almighty, look what the wind done blew in," Big Mama grunted. Mama was silent.

"Listen," Nate said to Big Mama, "I just come to help my Mama."

Big Mama laughed sarcastically. "Oh, listen to him all tough and smart mouthed. That's what's gonna get you killed, boy. That dirty mouth of yours."

He looked at Mama. "What's she talkin' 'bout?"

Big Mama made a high-pitched noise like a boiling teakettle. "Hoo whee, she done told me about what happened with the boss man. You lucky he didn't shoot you dead right there. You lucky if he don't take it out on your Mama or you brothers. We don't need that kind of trouble from the likes of you."

Nate suddenly felt ashamed. As much as he hated to admit it, Big Mama was right. He had put his family in danger, and now he was afraid—not for himself, but for Mama. He didn't care if Mr. Charlie killed him, but if anything happened to Mama because of what he had done, Nate could never forgive himself. His hands dropped from Mama's waist, and he backed out of the field. He went to the house and sat down on the porch stoop consumed by shame and fear. What had he done?

Later that afternoon he saw Mom Pearl heading toward his house. He ran up to greet her. "Poonie, come on over here and help your Grandma with this bucket." He looked up and saw Mom Pearl approaching. Just the sight of her calmed him. He jumped up, ran over, and grabbed a bucket full of fish from her hands as she struggled to balance her fishing pole. "Looks like fishin' was good today," he said.

"Yes, sir, it sure was," Mom Pearl said. She sat down on the porch with a groan. "But I am real tired. I want to leave some fish for your Mama, but I think I best rest a spell, too."

Nate offered to help her get her catch home and she gratefully accepted. "You just sit out here on the porch," he said. "I'll take care of the fish."

Mom Pearl groaned as she sat down on the top step. "Thank you, child," she told him. "You're a good boy."

After wrapping up a few fish in old newspaper and putting them in Mama's cooler, the two set out to walk the three miles to Mom Pearl's house.

Along the way, Nate's anxiety returned. Mom Pearl immediately sensed it. "Boy, somethin's buggin' you. Come on and tell your ol' Grandma what it is."

Nate shifted the fish bucket to his other hand. He felt too ashamed at first to tell her, but then the story came gushing from his lips. He described the hatred he had felt for Mr. Charlie, and the fear he now harbored that Mr. Charlie would retaliate by hurting Mama. Mom Pearl listened to her grandson, surprised by his boldness and the rage inside him. After what seemed like forever to Nate, she spoke. "What's done is done," she said. "You can't change it. But you get yourself to church on Sunday and ask God's forgiveness for what is in your heart. Ask for His help to heal yourself." Her voice quavered but remained very strong.

"Yes, ma'am I will. I've been prayin' already."

Mom Pearl wiped sweat from her forehead with the sleeve of her worn out work shirt. "That's good, child, that's good."

The two continued walking for another half mile. Nate trusted that God would forgive him, but he didn't know what the devil Mr. Charlie would do.

"Mom Pearl," he said, "what if Mr. Charlie tries to hurt Mama for what I done?" He looked into her eyes, almost afraid to hear her answer.

She paused and said, "Child, if he was gonna do somethin' he'd already have done it. But from now on just keep your head down, work hard, and be respectful. You learned your lesson. Don't make the same mistake again, child."

Nate stopped and threw his arms around her neck. "I won't Grandma. I'll be good from now on."

Mom Pearl laughed out loud. "Child you almost knocked me over."

The next day, Nate followed Mom Pearl's advice and prayed to God to forgive him during the service at Pleasant Star. As he prayed, he felt calmness come over him and tears welled up in his eye. He imagined that the Lord had touched him, and he vowed to work harder than ever and most of all to keep his mouth shut no matter what the devil said or did.

Chapter Sixteen

Mr. Redmond paced the sideline as his team practiced. He was concerned about his boys and understood the pressure they were under and the excitement they were feeling. In six days his team would be playing for the championship against Simmon High School of Hollandale, Mississippi. He couldn't hide the pride he felt for each of them. They were good boys who worked hard and kept their grades up at the same time. He wanted more than anything for them to bring home the trophy.

"All right, boys," Mr. Redmond shouted, "that's enough for today."

Nate took off his helmet and walked to the sideline. The other players were talking and laughing, but Nate mostly kept to himself. He walked straight over to Mr. Redmond. "Good practice, coach," Nate said to him.

"Thanks, son," the coach replied.

Son. Hearing that word from coach made him feel good and empty at the same time. He so desperately wished for a father and no one could have filled those shoes much better. He kept on walking and saw Chip sitting by the light pole a pile of schoolbooks surrounding him. "Hey, Chip," he said.

"You're gonna win on Friday. I know it," Chip told his friend.

"I hope so." Over Chip's shoulder Nate watched as Mr. Redmond's wife greeted her husband with a kiss on the cheek. Mr. Redmond hugged her and smiled, obviously happy to see her. His daughter ran up from behind her mother and hugged her father. Mr. Redmond picked her up and swung her around in the air. Such a happy, perfect family. "Why isn't my family like that?" Nate wondered. Absorbed by the scene, Nate forgot his friend was talking to him.

"Nate, I asked you if you was goin' home now. Hey!" Chip waved his hand in front of Nate's eyes and finally got his attention.

Nate was embarrassed. "Uh, yeah. I'll walk part way with you. Let me just change out of my gear."

As Nate walked toward the locker room, he saw someone approaching him from the corner of his eye. It was a tall dark figure. A man. He felt a prickly sensation run up the back of his neck and he stopped and turned to see who it was. The field lights reflected off the dark lenses of the man's sunglasses, and Nate froze. He knew who it was even though he had only seen this man a few times in his life. Although he had a strong impulse to run, Nate stood his ground as his father came up to him.

"Hi, boy."

Nate said nothing. What could he say to this man, his father whom he never knew? The silence was painful. Nate pulled at the laces on his shoulder pads.

"You're lookin' good out there," his father said.

"Thanks."

The elder Nathaniel just stared at his son, seemingly not knowing what else to say. Then he turned and walked away as inexplicably as he had appeared.

After gathering up his books, Chip caught up with Nate. "Who was that?" he asked.

Nate looked at his friend bewildered. "Huh?"

"I said, who was that?"

Nate started to walk toward the locker room. "Aw, that was nobody." He felt a twinge of guilt for lying to his friend, but then he realized he wasn't lying. His father was nobody to him, and it was clear Nathaniel Sr. would never become a somebody to his son. Awhile later Mom Pearl told Nate that his father and wife had moved away from Greenville, Mississippi. Nate barely cared. It would be many years before he would see his father again.

On Thursday, the day before the big game Nate began to feel ill, but he wouldn't let that stop him from practicing. Mr. Redmond noticed immediately that his star player wasn't himself. He questioned Nate, who told his coach he was fine.

When he got home after school, Mama was still at Miss Ann's doing her chores and cooking dinner for Mr. Charlie's family. Miss Ann was having a dinner party and had fretted for days over every detail. Mama returned each night exhausted. Miss Ann was extra hard on Mama with the big event approaching.

Nate so wanted to cook up a couple of squirrels he had shot the past weekend when he went hunting with Mr. Sylvester. Mama could use a nice dinner to keep her strength up. He tried to reach up to the ceiling where the meat was hanging, but he was overcome by dizziness. He felt awful. He had terrible chills and his head was pounding with pain. His whole body ached. Unaccustomed to being ill, he didn't know how to care for himself, and since no one else had cared for him in many years, he didn't quite know what to do. Finally, he decided to lie down on the stir mattress and sleep for a few minutes before starting Mama's dinner. His chores could wait until later, too. Wrapping himself in a blanket, he fell asleep.

"Boy, what in the hell are you doin' sleepin'?" Mama shouted, standing over him.

Nate's awoke with a start. Mama appeared out of focus to him at first. He rubbed his eyes and sat up.

Mama paced around the edge of the bed. "I can't believe I come home after workin' so hard all day and no dinner, no wood chopped. What the hell you doin'?"

Nate tried to stand up. "Mama, I'm sorry. I'll get to it. I fell asleep is all."

"Well, you better get you ass movin'. I works so damn hard and look what the hell I get."

Nate pulled on his jacket and went outside and chopped some wood. He started the fire in the stove and threw some squirrel meat into the pan to fry. Sweat rolled down his forehead and he felt like he would pass out, but he couldn't disappoint Mama. She had been working so hard.

As the two ate dinner, Mama talked on and on about how nasty Miss Ann had been to her. "Why, she made me polish that old silver serving tray three times 'cause she wasn't satisfied with how it look." Mama threw her head back and laughed. "I was 'bout ready to say wipe it yourself old woman but, thank the Lord, she told me it looked fine after the third cleaning."

Nate finished his dinner and started to wash the dishes. "Is James and Manual comin' home for dinner?" he asked.

Mama was chewing a big mouthful of meat, which she graciously finished before she spoke. "Naw, they's gone somewheres with Teenie. I don't expect them home too soon," she chuckled. She was proud of her other boys, who did what men were supposed to do, hangin' at the juke joint, chasing women, falling into bed well after midnight. Nate was the odd one. He never acted the way she hoped or expected. Instead, Nate talked nonsense about school and college and a career off the plantation when she needed him at home picking cotton and acting like a plantation man was supposed to act. Mama got up from the table and left the room. She never noticed how ill and struggling her son was that evening.

When he finished the dishes, Nate tended the fire in the stove. The nights that November were unusually cold. The family would need every bit of heat the old cast iron hearth could provide. As he walked to the other end of the house, he discovered Mama had already lay down on the stir mattress and fallen fast asleep. Nate gently positioned himself on the other side and quickly drifted off to sleep.

The next day he clearly felt no better than the day before. He could barely get himself out of bed and ready to meet the bus. He stood shivering at the bus stop. The morning dew had frozen on the tender tips of the straw grass. It would be a short growing season this year. More bad news for the Lowes. Making their quota would be almost impossible. Not that it would make any difference when settlement rolled around.

Nate dragged himself to his first class. Mrs. Williams took one look at him and sent him to the office. "You tell Mr. Williams to call Doctor. Jack. You need to see the doctor." Nate left his classroom, but he was too embarrassed to tell Mr. Williams to call Doctor. Jack for him. If he could just get some rest, he knew he'd be fine in time for the game. What could the doc do for him anyway? He sat down in an out of the way corner of the hallway, resting his tired back against the wall.

At lunch Mr. Redmond saw Nate sitting in the hallway his head down resting on his knees. He reached down and felt Nate's forehead. He was burning with fever. Mr. Redmond marched him into the office and called for a doctor's appointment. While they waited for the doctor to arrive, Mr. Redmond brought Nate some broth from the cafeteria. The warm liquid soothed him and made him sleepy. He lay down in the football dressing room. Rarely had anyone taken this much care over him. In spite of how sick he felt Nate smiled. He looked up at Mr. Redmond and said, "It's okay, Coach. I'm good to go."

Mr. Redmond looked serious. "Let's just wait and see what the doc says."

It took a long time for the doctor to arrive. Nate awoke after two hours and he still was not there. Mr. Redmond had gone to get the rest of the team ready for a prep meeting, which Mr. Redmond held before every game, especially one this important. The game against Hollandale was for the regional championship.

When Mr. Redmond returned to the dressing room, the doctor was examining Nate. Coach watched until the doctor finished.

"He's in bad shape. My guess it's pneumonia. If he plays tonight, he might collapse on the field," the doctor told Nate and Coach. "I'm gonna give him an injection of antibiotics. That should help some."

Nate was heartbroken. He wanted to play in the championship game. He didn't want to have to abandon his team when they needed him the most.

Coach sensed Nate's disappointment and wrestled with the idea of losing a key player on his team for the most important game of the year. "Son, do you think you can play?"

Nate sat up straight and tall. "Yes, coach, I think I can."

Mr. Redmond summoned the office secretary and told her to get some blankets. They wrapped Nate in the blankets and put him on the bus. At the game Coach Redmond wrapped Nate up snugly and sat him on the sidelines until it came time for him to play. As soon as he hit the field Nate's body forgot his illness, and he played as well as he ever had. The team won the championship, and they couldn't have done it without Nate. Everyone knew it, especially Coach Redmond. At the end of the game, he made sure Nate was wrapped up tightly in his blankets and walked him back to the bus. "Thanks for playing son. It made all the difference."

Coach's words were golden to Nate. While the rest of the team celebrated, Nate lay down on a seat at the back of the bus and fell into a deep, contented sleep.

At school the next week, Nate was a hero. Boys who had never talked to him now wanted to be his friend. Nate brushed them off and kept to himself as usual. Chip was so proud of his friend, laughing to himself as he watched the parade of attention that marched by Nate.

Along with the boys at school, girls wanted to get closer to Nate, too. That kind of attention made him very uncomfortable. As Nate and Chip sat outside during lunch, the prettiest girl at O'Bannon came over and sat next to Chip on the grass. She carefully pulled her pink skirt and petticoats under her as she sat. Chip and Nate immediately fell silent. Neither had ever imagined she would pay attention to them, but here she was.

Chip struggled to break the ice. "So, what'd ya think of Nate at the game on Friday?"

She smiled sheepishly, looked right past Chip and said, "I thought he was just wonderful."

Nate felt very uncomfortable. He began to feel a bead of sweat running down his forehead. Chip looked at his friend, confused by his silence. How could he not talk to her?

Without a word Nate got up and walked away. He simply didn't have time for the silly attention of the girls at school.

Reality soon returned to Nate's existence. Within a few months spring approached, and there was much work for him in the fields. He had work the whole acreage with little help from his family and had returned to check their progress and nurture the budding plants every day. Now was the time for pruning his crop. As he chopped the tiny green cotton plants to make the larger plants stronger, Nate sang his heart out in rhythm to his work. He sang an old spiritual that captured the pain that was inside him. Mom

Pearl's words had comforted him, yet he still worried about the kind of person he had become. How could he have wanted to kill a man, even the evil Mr. Charlie? Life on Mr. Charlie's plantation was nightmare enough to drive even the godliest man to violence or complete submission. Neither option was acceptable to Nate.

He ripped a few more tender shoots from the earth and cast them aside; many of the seeds planted had sprouted but now were unwanted, a nuisance to more hearty seedlings. The sun was hot for the early spring and sweat dripped from his brow and he was thirsty.

Wiping his forehead with an old blue bandana, he was determined to finish the field by nightfall. He tried to push on, but his mind raced and his heart ached. He stopped singing and stopped working. Standing in the middle of Mr. Charlie's cotton field, he turned his face to the sun and talked to God.

He felt warmth inside, and somehow he knew he would escape this life, that he would get off the plantation. He was infused with the conviction that in spite of all those who said he'd fail he would succeed. He reached down and picked up a handful of the cast off plants, pressed them to his nostrils and breathed in their fresh green scent. His life would take root and grow despite the curses and naysayers.

As night fell he finished the final row, and went home to sleep satisfied and refocused.

Chapter Seventeen

Although his friend Nate wasn't interested in girls, Chip could think of little else. He was a serious boy, but his teen years had changed the focus of his attention. At first Nate worried that Chip would falter in his schoolwork. He was careful to remind Chip of their dreams and goals whenever he feared his buddy had forgotten. It made Nate feel good to return the inspiration Chip had given to him. With a few choice nudges back to the business at hand, Chip managed to set his efforts on getting into college. Nonetheless, he remained in the quest for romance.

Nate wanted to keep to himself. He played sports, studied, worked in the fields, took care of Mama, and disappeared into a solo alcohol haze on the weekends. He had no time for a social life nor did he want one. Disappointed by the previous year's poor attendance and overall lack of participation in social activities, Mr. Williams, who Nate affectionately called Fess, sent out an edict that anyone who didn't attend that year's Junior/Senior Ball would be suspended for three days. The last thing Nate wanted to do was to go to the dance. He didn't care to stand around all evening feeling awkward and out of place, especially when he could be dead to the world after drinking a couple bottles of good old Orange Driver that he had stashed behind the outhouse. Nate did not go to the dance. Although he didn't think that Fess would follow through with his threat, Nate ended up with being suspended. He reckoned the embarrassment of the suspension was better than enduring an O'Bannon social event.

After several crushes and several rejections, Chip as the school year went on finally found a girl who returned his affection. Nate was relieved. He was growing tired of listening to Chips love lamentations. Unfortunately, his relief turned to dread when he heard what Chip had planned for him. Chip asked Jesse the girl he liked to go with him to the Senior Prom. She insisted that she would not go unless Chip found someone to go with her best friend, Ophelia.

Nate sat aghast across the lunch table from Chip. His friend had insisted that Nate join him inside for lunch and even shared a sandwich with him as a softening up measure.

Nate threw down his bologna on white. "Oh, no," he said, "Don't ask me. I aint gonna."

Chip in the throws of his crush would not give up easily. "Come on, please," he begged. "It's the only way she'll go. She likes me I know it. I'm sure I can get some. Come oooonnnn, man."

"Nah," Nate replied, "I can't, I just can't." He couldn't look Chip in the eyes.

"I promise, man, I'll owe you one big. Just do this for me, pleeease."

Looking up finally at his friend, Nate caught the look of longing and desperation in Chip's eyes. He struggled with the notion of the uncomfortable situation he'd be in if he agreed. Not much in his world seemed worse. But Chip was his best and only true friend.

Chip saw Nate was weakening. "Pleeeaase," he begged one more time for good measure.

A broad smile crossed Nate's lips. "Damn it. I done hate you sometime. All right, all right, I'll do it."

Chip shouted with delight.

Nate leaned forward across the table and grabbed Chip's shirt collar. "But you owe me——big."

The two boys laughed. "Yes, sir, I do. I really do," Chip told him.

The plan unfolded over the next few days. Nate would borrow a car from Teenie, and even though he didn't have a driver's license, Nate would drive so Chip and his girl could have the backseat. Nate and his "date" would occupy the front seat. "I'm gonna get me some," Chip proclaimed over and over. Nate was starting to get really tired of hearing it and wished the prom would come soon just to get it done with and behind him.

On the evening of the dance, Nate drove the beat up old Chevy he had borrowed to Chip's house to pick up the rest of his party. Chip wore a handsome black suit with a white shirt and a green tie. His date wore a frilly mint green dress. She looked like a bundle of colored cotton candy. Nate smiled as the two approached the car, looking very much in love.

Suddenly, whatever he would have to endure didn't seem so bad when he saw the bright smile on his friend's lips. "Good evening, Nate. How are you this fine night?" Chip asked as he helped his date into the car.

Nate chuckled at Chip's display of politeness, obviously designed to impress the young lady. But he played along. "I'm just fine, sir. And how are you?"

"Just dandy."

Nate glanced toward the passenger window and glimpsed a puff of pink crinoline. He jumped out of his seat and ran around to open the car door for his date. He had almost forgotten her as he watched the two lovebirds. Embarrassed by his lack of chivalry, he fumbled with the door handle, but opening it, he quickly recovered. "There you are. You look lovely tonight."

Ophelia giggled and got inside, smoothing her dress under her as she sat.

Nate wasn't lying. She did look quite beautiful. Still he wasn't interested in anything more than fulfilling his mission.

The dance was a great success. It was quite unlike anything Nate had ever seen before. The rickety gymnasium at the school was decorated with paper flowers and glittery stars. The lights were low and several teachers lurked in the shadows as chaperones. A rag tag band of old black men played big band tunes and love songs as the school kids danced in huddled pairs, slowly spinning in tight, little ovals. Chip and his girl Jesse danced all night. Nate and his date sat most of the evening at their table on the edge of the dance floor. Ophelia smiled politely, but she knew Nate was not interested in her. She leaned over to him. "Don't they look cute together," she whispered in his ear as they watched their friends dance.

"Yes, they sure do."

She touched his hand as it rested on the tabletop. "I'm glad we did this for them," Ophelia told him, smiling knowingly as she looked directly into his eyes without a bit of self-consciousness.

Nate understood. She was in the same boat as he was. He instantly relaxed. "Yes, me, too." They were in this together. From that moment, the rest of the evening flew by. He and his date talked and laughed as two friends, enjoying the gift they had given to some of the most important people in their lives.

After the dance, Nate drove around for a long time, allowing Chip and his girl to savor the delights of the backseat. He wasn't sure if Chip actually got some, but it sure sounded like they were enjoying themselves. Every now and then he'd glance over at Ophelia and share a quiet giggle with her over what they were doing. It was all right. He was pleased with himself.

In the weeks that followed the dance, Nate was hard at work on the cotton, his never-ending occupation and preoccupation. School was tough, but he had his now eternally grateful friend Chip helping him with gusto. Mama continued to work hard at Miss Ann's while her sons virtually raised themselves so over burdened was she by the demands of plantation life. Her boys were all men now in her mind. Even her youngest had taken to drinking and carousing with his older brothers Manual and Teenie. Around this time Teenie was between women and homes and started to live at Mama's house.

Teenie loved to wear Nate's clothes. After work he'd come to Mama's house and take a bath in a #3 aluminum washtub and get ready for an evening of drunken revelry with the ladies of the plantation. Wrapped in a blanket after his bath, he often went through Nate's clothes, picked out what he wanted and wore it without asking Nate's permission. Nate never said anything even though his clothes were his prized possessions. Over the years he had learned to fear his older brother, especially when he came home drunk. He was an ugly drunk who became argumentative with Nate and frequently punched and slapped his younger brother. Nate never fought back. That only would have made things worse.

One night Teenie wore Nate's beautiful beige vinyl jacket to the juke joint. Nate cringed as Teenie walked out the door with it slung over his shoulder. Uncharacteristically, Nate had splurged and paid a hard earned dollar for it one weekend while shopping with Chip in Glenallen. It looked so good he couldn't resist. And there was Teenie taking off with it, and Nate hadn't even gotten to wear it yet.

The next morning Nate found the jacket lying on the floor of the sleeping room. He picked it up quietly as Teenie lay snoring. Walking out onto the porch, he threw his errant jacket around his shoulders. As he did so, he noticed two tattered holes on the side bottom of the fabric. "What in the hell..." He was crushed but he didn't dare chastise Teenie for the damage to his beautiful garment.

Later after Teenie stumbled off to parts unknown, Mama sat on the porch crying. "What's the matter, Mama?"

Just then Manual and James stumbled into view from the back of the house. The two were laughing and Manual had his arm around James's neck. They came up and plopped down on the porch. "What's the matter, Mama?" James asked. The two boys had stopped laughing.

"It's Teenie. I swears that boy gonna be the death of me yet," Mama said through her sobs. She ran her hand along the side of her face and up into her hair, pushing back one of the three braids she wore on top of her head.

Nate watched her. She was starting to look so old, so tired. He wished he could do so much more for her. "What happened now?" he asked.

James and Manual fell against each other snickering.

Nate grew angry. "What's the matter with you two? Can't you see Mama's upset?"

The boys stifled their giggles.

Mama tried to compose herself. "It's all right. Leave them be."

Emanuel piped up. "We heard all about it."

"Yeah," said James, "my big brother just like a cat with nine lives. How many you reckon he got left?"

Manual laughed out laughed out loud and gave James a resounding high five.

Now Mama was angry. "You boys stop talkin' like that about your brother. He give me the death of fright."

It seemed that Nate was the only one who hadn't heard the

story of Teenie's latest exploit. "Will someone please tell me what happened?"

"Go on, Manual, you tell him. I can't talk about it," Mama said.

Manual stood up and faced the group on the porch. He enthusiastically acted out the story. It seems Teenie had gone after another man's woman as he had done so many times. The man, Bubby, went back to his house and came back with his gun. When he saw Bubby approach with the gun hanging out of his pocket, Teenie took off running. Bubby, who was quite drunk, pulled the gun out of his pocket. As he did so, the gun went off, nearly hitting him in his own foot. He managed to raise the gun and get off two shots before Jimmy Brook and Dave Mark subdued him and took away the gun. Amazingly the shots were very close to his mark, whizzing by Teenie's side and going right through the side panel of Nate's jacket, which flapped in the wind as Teenie high tailed it out of there.

James who had gone inside the house emerged with the damaged jacket. He held it up to the sun and examined the holes. "Woo weeee, they gone clean through."

Manual laughed and laughed while Mama sobbed. He went over to her and put his arm around her. "Come on, Mama. You gotta admit it sure is funny."

Mama stood up to escape his embrace. "No I don't. It aint funny. It aint funny no how." She marched into the house and slammed the door.

Manual hunched his shoulders. "Wooo hoooo," he cried, feigning fear.

He and Manuel collapsed against each other laughing.

"Damn, Nate, I wanted to wear this jacket of yours. It's nice," said Manual. "Guess that aint gonna happen now." He held it up and let the sun shine through the holes. The two boys were hooting and laughing again.

Nate started down the road. He was embarrassed by his brothers' behavior, all three of them. They were shameful to him. Everything seemed like a joke to them. Even Mama's pain and sorrow.

As reputation as a barber spread, Nate soon had a line of customers every other Saturday that twisted around the front of Mama's place and up the street to Sun Hall's house. They waited patiently and plunked down 50 cents a cut. Supply and demand had allowed Nate to double his price. So many of the plantation men wanted his services, Nate's haircutting skills were a hot commodity. Some barbering days Nate made over $35, which was more than he could make in a week picking cotton even on the best of days. A Nate Lowe cut became the fashion statement among the men of the Mr. Charlie's plantation and even on surrounding plantations. A good Negro barber was rare in those parts.

One Saturday, the line for haircuts was longer than usual. The afternoon was hot and sunny and the men waiting wiped beads of sweat from their foreheads with their shirt sleeves or bits of red or blue cloth handkerchiefs. Nate had set up a stool underneath the roof of Mama's porch and had a pitcher of weak unsweetened lemonade to refresh himself should the heat affect him. After awhile his hand ached from all the snipping of his scissors, but he kept on going. There was much money to be made. He had his eye on a pair of ladies shoes he had seen in a store in Glenallen. The moment he saw them who knew Mama would love them. He just had to make enough money to be able to afford them.

After a couple hours of cutting and old black ford drove up. LW Lott jumped out and ran over to talk to Nate. LW was a tall man about 6'2". He was a ladies man who always had to look good for the women folk. He didn't want to disappoint, so he was one of Nate's regulars. He showed up every time Nate set up his make shift barbershop.

"Damn, boy, you sure busy today." LW said, slurring his words. He looked a little unsteady on his feet. It was clear he'd had a few beers and maybe a couple of whiskey chasers. He was a hard drinker, rarely seen sober, but the men of the plantation liked him. He was a fun drunk, always making everyone laugh.

"Yep, that's true enough," Nate told him.

"Listen, boy, here's my 50 cents. I gots to go on up to Roy Shank's store, and I'm givin' it to ya now so's I don't spend it."

Nate looked at him funny. No one had ever done that before.

It took a few moments to see through the alcohol haze, but LW recognized Nate's confusion. "Don't worry, I'll be right back for my haircut, but since I paid in advance, I get to step right in for it when I come back, okay?"

Nate chuckled as he snipped stray hairs off the top and side of a nearly finished head. "Oh, I gets ya. You got some smarts goin' in that noggin of yours, you sure do," he laughed. "Okay then. You step right up when you gets back."

With that LW got into his car and drove off. "You're all done," Nate said to his latest customer and motioned for the one next in line.

An hour later Tump ran up to the house shouting about some car wreck about a half-mile up the road. Tump's big eyes were wide with shock. "There's a car in the ditch up there," he told Nate, "and someone's dead inside. I swear he's dead."

The line of customers broke up as the men ran up the road to see. Only the man Nate was already working on remained.

He, of course, wanted to get his money's worth before he went to see what had happened.

The men began to trickle back to Mama's house. They walked slowly shaking their heads. Horseman piped up and told Nate what he thought had happened. LW had left and gone up the road on his way to Roy Shank's store as he had told Nate. Inexplicably, his car left the dirt road and careened into a ditch. LW died instantly. He never made it back for his haircut "He sure enough dead all right," Horseman said his voice cracking. "His head all twisted back funny. Look like he broke his damn neck." Horseman pulled a rag from his pocket and wiped his eyes. LW left behind a wife and seven children.

Nate was stunned. He abruptly closed up shop for the day. As he swept the porch all he could think of was the bottle of Orange Driver waiting for him down by the lake bank. He drank the whole thing in one sitting and fell asleep for the night right there with the sound of the lapping of the lake against the banks filling his ears. For a young man who had seen so much death in his short life it was the only comfort to be found.

The next day the men of the plantation grieved the death of their friend. Tump took it especially hard. He sat leaning against the tree where the men had gathered. Hanging his head, he sobbed,

"He had too much to drink to drive right," he said. "I done told him not to do that."

Horseman sat down in front of Tump. "Now you knows how damn stubborn he was," he told his friend, trying to comfort him. "Weren't no way he gonna listen. We all tried to tell him."

"I knows it," said Tump. "I just gonna miss him so bad."

Nate wandered away from the scene and soon found himself on the lake bank. It wasn't long before he had drunk another bottle or two or three. He'd stopped counting. It didn't matter that it was Sunday and he was missing church. Mr. Syl had stopped by for him, but he made some excuse why he couldn't go. All Nate wanted was to be far away from his life and the liquor was working just fine.

Chapter Eighteen

Teenie stormed into Mama's house one day, shouting for his brothers. It was late May and Nate had just returned from the fields. James and Manual were sitting around back of the house by the old rusting carcass of a green Chevy that belonged to Teenie

Teenie walked through the house and out to the back yard. "Where the hell are you boys," Teenie yelled.

The brothers gathered round their elder sibling as he approached. Nate could see the anger in Teenie's eyes. In spite of all the pain Teenie had inflicted on him, Nate was concerned. "What's the matter, Teenie? You look like you could kill someone," he said.

"I aim to," Teenie said, "I aim to."

"What's you talkin' 'bout?" James asked.

"That bastard Pipe," Teenie said as he pushed down the hair on the side of his head, "he out to get me. He won't be happy until my ass is whipped from here to the state line."

Manual was angry now. "That son of a bitch."

Teenie sat down on the dirt and leaned his back up against the Chevy. He looked up into the sun and winced. "He gonna get his boys and come after me. I know it. But I aint afraid, no sir."

"I'll kick his ass," James said. "Just gimme a chance." James was eager for the opportunity to impress his eldest brother whom he idolized. He wanted to be just like Teenie—popular, smooth with the ladies, devil may care. His admiration caused him to pattern his life after Teenie. Teenie didn't go to school, didn't follow rules, got in trouble with the law. James would try to do the same.

Teenie stood up and pointed a finger at his brother. "Now you got somethin' there. Oh, yes you do." He rubbed his chin and smiled.

James smiled, too, but he tried to hide it. It wasn't often that his older brother paid so much attention to him.

Manual sat down at Teenie's feet. "What you mean?" Teenie laughed and straightened his sharp green jacket the ladies loved so much. "I mean he can't come after me. Not if I go after him first."

The Willie B boys slapped high fives all around. The rush of camaraderie made them feel strong, invincible. Even Nate was not immune. He felt it, too. The Willie B Boys were quite a force. Together they would stand and protect their own from outsiders who threatened them.

The levelheaded Nate, who had grown to hate violence of any kind since the day he meant to kill Mr. Charlie, was quite moved. In that instant of brotherly unity he forgot the church teachings his so loved and tried to live his life by. In an instant he decided. "Well, let's go then," he said. "Let's get the son of a bitch before he gets you."

James and Manual stood up a cheered, ready for a fight. James turned to the side and shadowboxed. Manual's face grew intense and focused.

Teenie held up his arms to get the boys attention. "Whoa, whoa, whoa," he said loudly. "Calm down. We best not run over there like a pack of wolves."

"What you mean?" Manual asked.

"Listen, we don't know what we's gonna find," Teenie told his cohorts. "We best get our guns. Just in case we run into somethin'."

The brothers agreed. Carried away by the mission, Nate did not even question what his brother had suggested. The boys became quiet now as they prepared themselves for what they had to do to protect their family.

Nate, Manual, and James went inside carefully checking first to make sure Mama wasn't home. She surely would not approve of what they were planning. The boys got their hunting guns and met Teenie at his car.

Teenie watched them as they approached—three young men

ready for business. He couldn't help but feel proud. "Look at you all. We gonna scare the pants off that bastard. Once he see me and my boys he aint gonna mess with me no more."

"Don't nobody wanna mess with the Willie B Boys," Manual shouted raising his rifle high in the air.

For an instant Nate thought, "Teenie's not takin' this serious at all. To him it's like a game or somethin' when we could end up killin' someone today." But he let that recognition pass through him and dissipate. He would be there to save his brother.

The boys piled into the car, and Teenie drove off headed for Rich's plantation where Pipe lived. They talked tough the whole way there. Making the most of his opportunity to impress Teenie, James was especially vocal, talking animatedly about how he was going to stand up to his brother's enemy and make him wish he'd never said anything bad about his brother.

Nate sat silent for most of the ride. He felt that old rage rising in him. All the disappointing settlements, the long, hard hours in the field for no reward, watching Mama work her fingers to the bone for Miss Ann. The anger and frustration bubbled just under the surface. He gripped his rifle, held it against his chest, and pointed it toward the roof of the car. The end of the barrel scratched the tan nylon cover and punched against the metal roof. His mind was filled with the pasty, thin face of Mr. Charlie, wizened and puckered up, yelling at him, at CW, at Mama. "No one messes with my family. No one messes with my family," he repeated over and over in his head like a mantra.

As they pulled into Rich's plantation where Pipe lived, they winded down the dirt and gravel roads in search of Pipe's plot. Teenie wasn't quite sure where it was. Then suddenly as they rounded a bend up ahead they spied a lone skinny old sharecropper on top of a green tractor with the unmistakable, long Prince Albert pipe jutting from his lips. It was their man.

Teenie stopped the car at the edge of the field and the four boys jumped out in unison, their guns pointing the way. Pipe saw them coming and panicked. He recognized Teenie leading the charge, and he was sure they were there to kill him. He wanted to run, but he knew he'd never escape. Teenie walked toward the cowering man, yelling and screaming at him, berating and challenging the old man sitting on the broken down field machine. "What you mean talkin' 'bout me all over? Who the hell you think you are, boy?" Teenie shouted.

James stepped up. "Yeah, who you think you are?"

Pipe looked down at them from his perch atop his tractor. "I don't know what you're talkin' 'bout," he said his voice seemed choked in his throat. Nate watched him carefully. Pipe was shaking visibly. This wasn't who Nate had pictured when Teenie described his tormentor. From Teenie's words he envisioned a swaggering young buck with a big mouth that caused trouble for Nate's family for sport. Pipe seemed like a humble man advanced in years just driving his tractor to provide for his family. "This all feels so wrong," Nate thought. Maybe it was his church going or just plain good sense, but he suddenly wanted to leave. They had done what they had come to do. The fear of God had been put into him. That was enough, more than enough.

But Pipe's protestations had the opposite affect on his brothers. They shouted back at him, especially James and Manual, who hadn't actually heard anything that Teenie claimed Pipe had said about him around Lake Jackson. Nate watched them in fear. His brothers' rage grew with each passing minute. It seemed they would not be happy until blood was spilled.

Pipe held his hands up and lowered them down slowly. "Boys, come on now. This is all just a misunderstanding. I didn't mean no harm."

Teenie stepped right up to the tractor and looked Pipe straight in the eyes. "You a damn liar," he said. "Come on down here and face me like a man."

Pipe stayed put on his perch. At his age he knew he was no match for a strapping young man like Teenie, let alone his three brothers. "Teenie, listen to me," he begged, "I'm a father and my little girl is pregnant. I just want you to do right by her. That's all I ever said. She's my baby girl. I love her with all my heart." Pipe started sobbing.

Nate watched him closely and knew instinctively that he was sincere. He also knew his daughter, a real beauty who couldn't have been more than sixteen years old. He took a few steps back from his comrades and lowered his gun barrel. Teenie was thirty-one and he had gotten that young girl pregnant. Nate winced. No wonder Pipe was upset with Teenie. He had every right to be.

Teenie raised his gun toward the sky. "Yeah, well that don't give you no right to talk shit about me, do it?"

Manual stood beside Teenie, glaring at Pipe. "Let's beat the livin' crap out of his ass," he said.

"Yeah," said James, still trying to impress his older brothers. "I'll kick your ass old man."

Pipe shivered with fear. "Look, I'm sorry," he said. "I didn't mean nothin'. I'm sorry."

"You best mean that," Teenie said, "If I ever hear you said another bad word about me, we'll be back. You can bet on that."

Teenie turned and walked toward his car. James and Manual followed backing away with their eyes trained on Pipe as if to underscore and support Teenie's threats. Nate stood for a minute watching Pipe. The old man looked like he could hardly breathe. Nate wanted to say something, to apologize, but the word lodged in his throat crammed down by the shame he felt.

"Nate, what the hell you doin'?" yelled Teenie. "Let's go."

Nate turned and ran back to the car. The entire ride home Teenie, Manual and James laughed and boasted about the experience. "Did you see his face when he saw us?" Teenie said. "I thought he was gonna shit in his pants."

"I think he did," said James, laughing so hard he could barely speak.

Nate stared out the window. He had never been so ashamed of his family or himself. He vowed he would never go along with them on anything ever again. He promised himself over and over again that he would not be like them, not in any way. Not ever.

Teenie never did right by Pipe's daughter. She gave birth to the child, and Teenie gave them no acknowledgement or support.

June arrived and Nate's last days of high school raced by. While the other students were going to parties and cutting class, Nate was more serious than ever. Soon he would be the first of his entire family to graduate, and he wanted to savor the work of finishing his classes with his goal within his grasp. He had completed what he had started, a feat that no Lowe before him could accomplish. As he sat outside leafing through his history book studying for his last test of the year, he mused about the trail of drinking, lost hope, and suffering that made up his family tree. A wide smile opened up on his face. He already was different.

Graduation day was a whirl of excitement. Nate felt better than he had in his entire life. No one ever gave him a chance. No one ever believed in him on the plantation. They all thought he was crazy. Even Doctor Jack had said it. No one on the plantations bothered to disbelieve or help or encourage him. He had done it all on his own with the help of wonderful teachers, coaches, and his best friend Chip.

Nate sat with his classmates on the playing field behind the high school. He wore his favorite dark blue suit with fine thin lapels, his white cotton dress shirt, and a blue and green tie. He looked sharp. Ophelia had told him he looked better than he had on the night of the prom. She had motioned to him to lean closer and she whispered in his ear, "I'm so proud of you." Chip had vigorously shook Nate's hand. "We did it, man," he exclaimed. "We did it." Nate had just smiled and took his place in the rows of seats for the graduates.

Just before the speaker began, Nate turned around and scanned the gathered family and friends of his classmates. He searched for a familiar face. He didn't expect any of his family to be there. Mama said she had to work in the fields and at Miss Ann's, but she'd try to make it. Surely, this would be another time when no one came to support him.

The speaker rose and stood before the wooden podium. There was no microphone so he had to speak loudly to be heard. He told the graduating class to look forward and achieve. "Young people," he said, "This is just the start. You have just begun. You have made the start, but what good is it if you don't finish." Nate listened closely but grew impatient as he waited for his name to be called. He just wanted to feel that diploma in his hands. This was the proudest moment of his life thus far. The joy he felt was immeasurable.

Watching his classmates ascend to the stage one by one, he

waited feeling like his heart would burst. Finally, he heard his name and walked onto the stage. Fess, Mr. Williams, shook his hand and winked at him. Nate turned and faced the crowd.

He raised his diploma in the air and shook it. He had never been so happy. As he walked toward the edge of the stage to return to his seat, he smiled at the crowd.

Suddenly toward the back of the aisle he saw Mama. She was jumping up and down and smiling with pride. She clasped the shoulders of the woman in front of her. "That's my boy," she cried. "That's my boy." Her voice was so loud the whole crowd heard her and turned to look. Nate was mortified. Everyone saw her. Mama with her hair up in a rag, dress dirty, face all shiny from sweating in the sun. She'd come right from the fields. She didn't even bother to fix her hair or wash up. Nate felt so ashamed. He slid down into his seat and lowered his head and clasped his hands together. "Lord," he prayed silently, "please don't let me turn out like my family. Please let there be more in life for me. Please." But at least Mama was there. It was the first time he could remember that she had come to any event to support him.

Chapter Nineteen

After graduation Nate felt his dreams slipping away. Mama put pressure on him to work the fields, to pick as much cotton as he could, and Nate obeyed her. Standing in the cotton field one day, he put down his cotton sack, fell to the ground and cried. He began to believe he would never get off the plantation.

The sun beat down on his back. Sweat poured from his forehead. He looked around and saw twenty men and women working their plots for Mr. Charlie. Their backs were bent in unnatural arcs. A few of them were singing to Jesus. "Where the hell is Jesus," Nate shouted. "Where the hell are you, Lord? You sure aint helpin' me none. No, sir."

Mama came running over from three rows away. "Boy, you quiet down, now," she whispered sternly. "You actin' all crazy again. Stop it." She wiped her neck with a rag. She looked so old, so tired. Her hands were cracked and blistered. As quickly as she had run up, she sallied away as if she did not want to be seen with Nate. He watched her go, dragging her half empty cotton sack behind.

Nate stood up and returned to his work. It all felt so futile. When he was younger, he dreamed of working hard and getting a settlement at the end of the year. But he was twenty years old now and a high school graduate. He knew no matter how hard he worked a settlement would never come his family's way. Mr. Charlie had decided long before not to favor the Lowes. He worked mechanically, filling one sack and then another until his fingers started to bleed.

Just as the light was about to pass away, a dust cloud rose in the distance. A car approached. He recognized Mr. Williams's baby blue

Buick Le Sabre, the sun glinting off the chrome. The car stopped at the edge of the Lowe crop. The setting sun shone in Nate's eyes, but he could make out two men approaching. It was Mr. Redmond and Mr. Williams. Nate wondered what they were doing there only a week after graduation.

The two men greeted Nate. They asked him how it felt to be a high school graduate.

"It feels real good," said Nate, although that wasn't quite the truth. The excitement of graduation day had worn off as he slid back into plantation life and saw no clear path to his future.

Mr. Redmond clapped his hand on Nate's shoulder. "You should be very proud, young man."

Mr. Williams rubbed his chin and looked at Nate with a troubled glare. "What are you going to do now?"

Nate felt uncomfortable. He didn't want to answer but under the watchful eyes of his teachers he had no choice. "I don't know, Fess."

The two men looked at each other and shook their heads. "Son, you need to go to college. It would be such a crime if you ended up spending the rest of your life on this plantation," said Mr. Williams.

"Yes, it certainly would be," added Mr. Redmond.

Nate felt the tears of his confusion welling in his eyes. He knew they were right. "But Fess, I just don't know what to do. My Mama needs me here. I feel like I can't leave her alone."

"Son, you know the only real hope your Mama has of getting a better life is you getting off the plantation. Go to college, build yourself a career, make the money you deserve, and then you can help your Mama," Mr. Williams told him. "Staying here means you both will be like slaves for the rest of your lives, always just getting by, always struggling."

Nate stood silently, staring at the ground.

Mr. Redmond stepped up to him, lowered his head and caught Nate's eyes. "Son, you know he's right," he said. "Now what are you going to do?"

"I know some people at Arkansas A&M," Mr. Williams told him. "I'm sure they could get you in there."

Nate shuffled his feet. He felt so uncomfortable. He knew Mama would be devastated, but he also knew what his teachers said was the truth. The only chance he had was to get off the plantation. "That's where Chip's goin', aint it?"

Mr. Redmond smiled. "Yes it is," he said. "Mr. Williams got him in there and he can do the same for you. All you gotta do is say yes."

Mr. Williams put his hands in the pockets of his khaki dress pants and leaned back on his heels. "And don't worry about money. I can get you on a work-study program. All your expenses will be paid."

Nate winced. His dream was right in his grasp. Yet there was one troubling obstacle. "I want to go," Nate told them, "but my Mama, she needs me. I don't think I can leave her. She'd never understand."

"Don't you worry none," Mr. Redmond assured him. "We'll talk to her."

The two men went back to the house with Nate and waited until Mama returned from her evening chores at Miss Ann's. She was not happy to see them. This was not the first time they had come to talk to her, and she knew what they were wanting.

Mr. Redmond and Mr. Williams talked with Mama for two hours. In the end she acquiesced, but only because she was tired and didn't want to argue anymore. The two men knew her approval was half hearted at best, but they saw their opening and took it. Leaving the plantation, they assured Nate that he would be enrolled at Arkansas A&M by the next morning. Nate was instructed to stop by O'Bannon to pick up his papers. "I'll take care of everything," said Mr. Williams.

The next day Nate stopped by Chip's house and told him the news. Chip was ecstatic. "We're gonna be college boys!" he shouted. "I knew we'd make it. I knew we would."

By mid-August Nate would have to report to campus. He and Chip were going together, triumphantly. Nate was very excited. Nonetheless, he felt tremendous guilt about leaving Mama alone. Teenie was off on his own chasing trouble and women wherever he could find them. James and Manual never really picked cotton.

Both were too spoiled and Mama let them go. He feared none of his brothers would help her. Mama would be all alone to support herself and her selfish sons. "Selfish, yeah my brothers is selfish," Nate thought as he swept the front steps on a steamy day in late July. "but aren't I selfish, too. I'm leaving Mama for my own selfish reasons." He stopped and leaned the ratty broom against the house. "Maybe I'm the most selfish one of all."

Around that time Big Mama moved in with Mama. Her health had been failing, and Paw Paw and she had finally separated after 42 years of marriage. Paw Paw was a good man, but he was a drunk. He was a happy drunk. Quiet and reserved when he was sober, he was quite the opposite when he drank. Down at the Green Frog, he drank corn whiskey and laughed and danced and flirted with women. He was not the kind who would ever cheat on his wife as many plantation men routinely did. He was just having a good time. Big Mama could never abide his behavior. Year after year, she nagged and accused him. Finally, Paw Paw had enough, and he left her once and for all.

After Paw Paw left, Big Mama became more bitter and angry. Her health deteriorated. The few times she had seen Dr. Jack he had told her she had high blood pressure. He gave her some pills to calm her and advised her to take it easier. She, of course, didn't listen. Like her Mama before her, she relied on home remedies. For high blood pressure she mixed a cocktail of Epsom salts and grapefruit juice and drank some every day.

Mama had urged her for some time to move in, but Big Mama refused. One day she fell in her house and couldn't get up. Forty-eight hours later Mama found her lying in the same spot where she fell. Uncharacteristically, Mama laid down the law to Big Mama. She was coming to live with her and that was that.

By the time she moved in Big Mama's health had gotten so poor she was confined to bed for most of the day. Nate felt bad for her and tried to make her as comfortable as he could. He soon found out her ill health had not dampened the fire of her tongue nor her need to constantly berate him. Big Mama made it clear she thought Nate's going to college was about the funniest joke she had ever heard. Laughed so hard she could barely speak she'd say, "College, what the hell you gonna go to college for? I declare you are the biggest, laziest brat I have ever seen. Leavin' your Mama like that. And for what? For nothin' that's what."

When Big Mama fell asleep Nate would steal a few more of her nerve pills. Shortly after he swallowed a few, nothing seemed so bad, not his guilt over leaving Mama, the wrath of his grandmother, his fear of leaving home in spite of his desires, nothing. It was the only time he really felt happy. He soon had developed quite a liking for those nerve pills.

Soon the time came for Nate to leave for college. Chip was excited, but Nate was apprehensive. Mama cried and cried the day he packed up his few belongings and left the plantation. He couldn't bear her tears, so he promised her he'd be back. As he sat in his tiny dorm room, he couldn't get Mama's pleading tears out of his mind. He felt homesick, yet he knew he had to get away, to get off the plantation. But Mama needed him so bad. Despite the hardship and toil, he missed the only life he'd ever known.

It did not take long for Nate to realize he did not like Arkansas A&M. The campus seemed large and unfriendly. He found it difficult to concentrate in class, so he missed most of the content of the lectures he attended. His work-study job he was to milk the cows on the campus dairy farm. Of all the jobs he had done in his life he without a doubt most hated milking cows. He was ashamed and felt more like a slave than he ever had on the plantation. He needed something to dull his pain, and he began to make regular trips to the general store across from campus to buy some good old Orange Driver. After a bottle or two was the only time he felt all right.

Chip, on the other hand, took to college life immediately. He loved his classes, making friends, joining clubs and socializing. He had even met a young lady named Gail he very much admired. The only dilemma he face was how to break up with Jesse, but he soon did that via a long apologetic letter. Soon he and his new girl were inseparable and very much in love. Even in the whorl of his happiness and newfound freedom, Chip couldn't help but notice his friend's misery.

One night several weeks into the semester Nate came to Chip's room. He told his friend he wanted to leave school. It simply did not feel right to him. Without hesitating, Chip gave Nate enough money to buy a bus ticket. Nate thanked him over and over again and apologized for letting him down.

"Don't you worry," Chip said, "just find another school where you can get your degree. Don't give up on our dreams." Nate promised he would, but he knew he might never realize his own dream.

Nate bought a bus ticket and went back home. Mama was happy to see him and immediately put him to work sweeping the floors. "Aint no good for my Mama to be breathin' in all this dust and dirt," she told him. "Get on in there and clean it up."

He obeyed his Mama. He swept up the front room where the kitchen was and the back room where the meat was hung for curing, deliberately avoiding the sleeping room where Big Mama held court. Finally, he had to go in there and face her. Much to his surprise, she didn't say a word. Just an "Uh huh" when she saw him. Nate tried not to look at her but the haughty smile on her face burned a hole in his mind. Her expression didn't change until he left the room. It felt worse than her longest most abusive tirade against him. The grunting I-told-you-so and the who's-eating-crow-smile left him reeling. He put down the broom, ran out back, and vomited.

He sat down on a patch of dried grass and held his head in his hands. Hot tears welled up in his eye. "Lord, tell me what I gotta do," he shouted. But no response came. He had never felt so alone. He wanted a drink or some pills but he had none. There was no comfort to be found.

As the week dragged on he resolved that if he couldn't go to school he'd find a job. Anything to get himself off the plantation. Anything. One morning he left the house before sun up and hitchhiked into Jackson. After three days he found a job on a construction site. He mostly carried lumber from one end of the job site to the other. It was hard work, but he liked it fine. The money was decent; he got off the plantation and was far from Big Mama's poisonous influence and Mama's discouragement.

After Nate was on the job about four weeks, he had settled into a routine and was quite comfortable. His weekends were a blur of alcohol and Big Mama's nerve pills, but he always made it to his job on Monday morning on time and ready to work. That day a new guy named Miles started working the site. The foreman introduced him to Nate and the two said a quick hello. At lunchtime he heard the seasoned workers joking about how inexperienced Miles was. While Nate was assigned to more or less work odd jobs on the site, the foreman had sent Miles to work with the actual construction of the building, and he was beginning to slow down the regulars. They were lighthearted about it now, but Nate didn't envy him. He knew that after awhile they would begin to dislike Miles and make life difficult for him.

After a couple of days on the job, Miles was trying feverishly to earn the respect of his co-workers. Nate didn't care what the others thought, but Miles did. Trying to make a good impression, Miles worked extra hard, but he often made mistakes. He sat down next to Nate during lunch break and didn't say a word. He ate his cheese sandwich and stared at the building. Nate thought the poor guy looked as though he were going to cry. "Looks pretty good," Nate said to get Miles mind off his troubles with some small talk.

"Huh," Miles said and turned and looked directly at Nate. He had very large, soulful dark eyes that looked right through Nate.

"The building, looks like it's comin' along pretty good," Nate said smiling.

"Oh, uh huh." Miles looked away and went back to his sandwich.

When the lunch break was over the two men returned to their work without saying another word to each other. The foreman had told Nate he needed to unload a truck full of concrete brick and bring them to the north side of the building. Although he'd been working on it steady since early morning, it was three o'clock and he was only about halfway through. His hands were raw and bleeding. He didn't have any work gloves and couldn't afford to buy any for himself, so he had to endure.

As Nate headed back to the truck for another load, he heard a shout coming from the inside of the skeleton of the building. "Oh my God, boss, Miles done fell off the building," one of the men screamed. "He fell down three stories."

Nate ran back. The foreman rushed by him and stopped. Nate stood next to him. "Nate, go on in there and check on Miles. See if he's okay."

Although he didn't want to go, Nate followed his boss's order. He wove his way in among the wooden beams and there at the center he saw Miles' body on the concrete foundation. Blood was flowing from his nose and his head was crushed. Nate knelt down next to Miles. He reached over and closed his dull, lifeless eyes. The unfortunate man had been working on the upper floors and in his haste and desire to please and impress had lost his balance and slipped. It was an error in judgment that cost him his life.

Nate emerged from the building and reported to the foreman, who turned around to call the authorities to have the body removed. No one shed a tear for Miles. The men milled around until the body was taken away, and then they all went back to work. Except for Nate. Sitting on the edge of the pick up he was supposed to be unloading, he blinked back tears as he thought of Miles, but he soon realized he was crying more for himself. He jumped down from the truck and went over to the foreman's shack. "Boss, I gotta talk," Nate said.

The foreman looked up from his plans. He already knew what Nate was going to say. "All right, sit down," he said pulling over a rusty metal chair.

"Nah, that's okay," Nate told him. "Boss, I gotta go. I can't work here no more. I just can't."

The foreman stood up and put his hand on Nate's shoulder. "Well, I'm sorry to see you go. But I understand." He grabbed some bills from a dented cash box, counted out Nate's pay and handed it to him.

Nate half smiled. "Thank you, boss." With that he turned and walked away and never came back.

Chapter Twenty

Riding home on an old Greyhound bus, Nate made a solemn vow to himself. He would not stay long on the plantation. He leaned his head back against the blue gray seat. When he was in high school things seemed so simple. Dreaming was so easy. The reality of being on his own in the world was far more difficult than he could have imagined. He began, curiously, to understand why Mama was so bound to the plantation. Life there may have been difficult and unfair, but it was regular and unchanging. The only challenges were expected ones, the obstacles familiar, even comfortable.

The bus pulled into the station in Hollandale and Nate emerged into the humid summer air. Heading out to the highway, Nate hitchhiked the thirty miles to the plantation, all the time dreading Big Mama's mean spirited reception that was unchanging, but never comfortable.

When he arrived home, he was surprised to find Big Mama silent. She lay in bed almost unable to move. Mama rushed up to him and hugged him. She seemed genuinely happy to have him home again. Nate told her nothing of what he had encountered in the outside world, knowing it would only scare her. Mama stood before him smiling broadly dressed in an old work shirt and work pants, her hair tied up in a rag. She hugged him a second time. "I'm so glad you're home," she said. "We can raise some cotton now that you're back."

Nate looked down at his mother who looked nearly a foot shorter than he. "Mama, come on," he said, "let's not talk about that now. I just got home." He didn't have the heart to tell her his plans.

"Oh, you go on," Mama smiled, being unusually playful she shoved Nate's arm. "We got lots of plannin' to do if we gonna get some harvest in."

"Mama, stop."

Mama laughed. "No, you stop. Let's go on out to the field right now for a look-see. I wanna know what you think we can still do before harvest is over." Cotton was the only life she knew. She was eager to reclaim it.

Nate turned away from her.

"What's the matter, son?"

Nate faced her and looked her in the eyes. "I can't, Mama, I just can't."

Mama was genuinely surprised. "What you mean?"

He took her hand and spoke gently but firmly. "I can't stay. I've got to be movin' on."

Mama clasped her hand over her mouth and began to cry.

"Mama, don't cry," Nate told her. "I'm gonna make a better life for both of us. You'll see. I don't know how, but I swear to God I'm gonna."

Mama turned and ran out of the house sobbing. Nate felt horrible. She was the last person he ever wanted to disappoint. As he turned to put his bag into the sleeping room, Big Mama watched him. He glanced straight at her. She just glared at him, her mouth stretched out in a crooked smirk.

The next day was Sunday, and the family was listening to a popular Christian radio program called the Toboring Hour. Nate's former teacher Mr. Carter hosted the program. Mama brought the tiny battery powered transistor radio into the sleeping room so Big Mama could hear it. The sound quality was poor and scratchy, but they knew no different and paid close attention to every word Mr. Carter uttered and enjoyed the beautiful church music he played. Even Big Mama wore a rare pleasant expressions as a choir sang, "Nearer My God To Thee." Nate sat on the floor and leaned up against the wall across from her. Mama milled around with a broom, sweeping here and there, getting rid of her nervous energy on her only day off. The choir finished singing and the last piano chords faded.

"And now time for some announcements," Mr. Carter said. "Sarah Davis has passed away in Clarksdale, God rest her soul. She leaves no survivors but for a sister. The woman who cared for Miss Sarah in her last days tells us her sister's name is Callie McDaniel. We believe she lives somewhere around Lake Jackson."

Mama gasped and Big Mama clasped her chest. "Thas my sister," she managed, slurring her words. "Thas my sister."

Nate, too, was surprised, but he shushed the women, so he could hear the rest. "If anyone knows the whereabouts of Miss Callie McDaniel, please call the station for more information."

Mama began to cry. She remembered well her Aunt Sarah, who was always kind to her. Big Mama and Aunt Sarah were half sisters. Aunt Sarah's father was white. The two had been fairly close as children, but as Big Mama grew more ornery with age, the two stopped speaking and soon lost touch completely.

Big Mama began to breathe heavily. "Oh my Lord, my sweet Lord, my poor sister's dead," she wailed. "Oh my sister, my sister." She sobbed uncontrollably.

Mama rushed over and tried to calm her. "Now, Mama, hush now. You shouldn't be getting all in a tizzy." Big Mama continued to wail and when she tried to get up from her bed, she fainted. Nate ran to the water basin and made a cool rag and put it on her forehead. Mama gingerly slapped her cheeks to bring her around. When she came to, Big Mama was calmer, but still very distraught. "Well, someone's gotta go on up there to Clarksdale and take care of things, but I's too sick to go take care of my sister," she said and broke down sobbing.

Nate rushed over to her side. "Don't worry," he said, "I'll go and take care of everything."

"You do that," she said without an ounce of gratitude. "Someone's got to and it may as well be you."

Nate picked up his jacket and headed out the door undeterred by his grandmother's ungratefulness. He had to do this task. It was his duty to his family. For him there was no question or second thought.

Nate got into one of Teenie's old Chevys and drove into Lake Washington to Roy Shank's General Store. He used the pay phone inside and called the radio station and got the information he needed. The voice on the line told him to go to Clarksdale and see a woman named Miss Piggy, who had cared for Aunt Sarah up until her death.

Later that day Nate drove to Clarksdale and went to Miss Piggy's house. She was very glad to see him, and talked on and on about what a good God fearing lady his Aunt was. Miss Piggy was quite influential in the Negro community in town. Secretary of the local chapter of the NAACP, an organization nearly unheard of on Mr. Charlie's plantation, she was a businesswoman who ran her own beauty salon. Petite with dark chocolate skin, she was well dressed in a green ruffled dress with matching earrings and necklace. She even wore hose, and her hair was fixed up in an upsweep on top of her head. Her house was quite spacious and neat as a pin, filled with polished wood furniture and comfortable sofas and chairs. Nate had rarely seen such luxury in a Negro's house. As she spoke he couldn't help but fantasize that one day he would have such a place to live in.

"Well," Miss Piggy said chuckling, "I should stop running my mouth and take you down to Sarah's place."

Nate nodded. "Yes, ma'am, if you would be so kind."

"Oh," Miss Piggy replied. She was already very impressed by this polite young man.

Miss Piggy walked Nate down to Aunt Sarah's home a few blocks away. He was silent on the walk while Miss Piggy talked about Aunt Sarah's sweet nature and generosity with the little she had. Suddenly, her voice was lost in the wail of a railroad horn, blaring over and over. Nate looked over at her as she walked next to him. Her lips were moving, but he could not hear a sound she uttered. The ground began to shake under his feet and the rush and clamor of the locomotive whooshed right behind the tiny house they were approaching. Digging into her shiny black pocketbook, Miss Piggy pulled out a tarnished brass key. She opened the front door of the little brown wooden dwelling.

Motioning for Nate to enter she stepped aside and waited outside to give him time to be alone and grieve. Without thinking Nate walked straight down the hall to the back of the shotgun house. He stood in Aunt Sarah's bedroom and looked out the white curtained window. The railroad track was only a few yards from where he stood. Turning he faced the front door and surveyed what Aunt Sarah had left behind from her quiet life. There were lots of clothes, church dresses and work dresses and aprons, spring coats and winter coats, shoes, hats, and purses. A plain wooden crucifix was hung over her black iron bed. On her dresser were carefully positioned family pictures. He picked up on frame with a portrait of two teenage girls, dressed in their Sunday best, looking quite uncomfortable at being photographed. Their bodies were stiffly posed, their faces unsmiling like someone had forced them to take the picture. The younger girl on the right leaned against the other and tightly held on to her hand.

"Ahhh, she loved that picture," Miss Piggy said, walking up behind him. "It's the only picture she had with your grandmother."

"That's Big Mama, uh, I mean, my grandmother?"

Miss Piggy took the picture from him and held it out at arms length to catch the light from the window. "Yes, that's her right there," she replied, pointing to the younger girl. "She didn't want to have her picture took. She thought it was the devil's work, but Sarah, she begged and begged, and sure enough Callie agreed, but just that one time."

Big Mama looked so youthful and innocent, so trusting of her older sister. Nate was amazed at this glimpse of his grandmother's past. Her eyes looked almost kind and wondering. What had happened to make her lose that innocence and trust? What had happened to estrange the sisterly bond so evident in the photo?

Nate stopped himself from his thoughts and returned to the task at hand. He asked Miss Piggy where he could fetch some boxes and he packed up the clothes and pots and pans and dishes. He loaded them and an old icebox and a few pieces of furniture into the back of Teenie's car. With Miss Piggy's assistance he took care of all of Aunt Sarah's debts with the money he had made on the construction job. He closed all of her affairs without thought or question, and he made the arrangements and paid for her funeral. It was the responsible thing for her relative to do.

His behavior did not go unnoticed. Miss Piggy was very

impressed by him. He drove her back to her home when he was finished and parked out front. She invited him inside and offered him a glass of iced tea. "You go sit on the settee," she said, directing him to the red sofa in front of the picture window. Nate sat down, a bit nervous, wondering if his clothes were dirty from the packing. He did not want to soil her fine furniture.

She returned from the kitchen with blue glass tumblers and handed one to Nate. He took a long drink, being quite thirsty from a long afternoon of laboring over Aunt Sarah's affairs. He moved to put his glass down on the coffee table, but stopped not wanting to leave a watermark on Miss Piggy's coffee table. She quickly slid a wooden coaster under his glass and bade him set his glass down. She sat down across from him on a wooden rocking chair.

She reached over and touched the top of his hand as it rested on his knee. "You are a fine young man to do all this for your Aunt," she told him. "You are strong and responsible."

"Why, thank you, Miss Piggy," he said a little embarrassed. "I did what I had to do."

Miss Piggy leaned back in her seat. "A young man like you should be going to college," she said. "Where are you going to school?"

Nate reluctantly told her of his abortive experience at Arkansas A & M. He sincerely hoped she would not think less of him. Already he had come to respect her and wanted her approval and acceptance.

When he had finished his story, she looked him straight in the eyes and leaned forward. "I understand, child. It's very hard, but you can't let one bad time stop you. You gots to go on with your dreams."

"I want to, very much," Nate said his voice cracking with emotion. "I feel so strongly I needs to, but I just don't know how."

Miss Piggy looked at him and smiled. "I can help you," she said. "Let's go see a friend of mine."

She got up and grabbed her pocket book from the hall table. Nate didn't move, unsure of what she was doing. "Come on," she said, "do you want to go to college or not?"

Nate rose to his feet. "Yes, ma'am, I surely do," he answered firmly, but I don't have no money and I don't know what to do." He felt scared and uncertain.

"Don't you worry," Miss Piggy said. She walked over and touched his shoulder. "All you have to do is want to and we'll take care of the rest."

The two got into Teenie's car and Miss Piggy directed him to drive to Stranger's Mortuary. Inside the old Victorian house that smelled of mothballs and lye soap Miss Piggy introduced Nate the Mr. Stranger the proprietor. He was a tall, very dignified looking gentleman. Nate later learned he was also very active in the local NAACP. Miss Piggy told him about Nate. "It's a crime that such a fine young colored boy isn't in college," Miss Piggy exclaimed.

Mr. Stranger knew Miss Piggy was not easily impressed. Her recommendation of Nate was one to be taken seriously. "It would be a crime, that's true, Miss Piggy," he agreed. "I know just what we should do about that."

Miss Piggy smiled. "I knew you would, I just knew you would."

The trio jumper into Mr. Stranger's car, he drove them to Cohoma Junior College where he and Miss Piggy had good friends in high places. When they arrived at the college, Nate, Miss Piggy and Mr. Stranger were ushered right into the office of the president, Mr. McLauren. An elderly gentleman he was in his last year as the head of the school. He stood up and shook Nate's hand. Miss Piggy was a longtime friend of his and once he had heard her opinion of Nate no time was wasted in finding a way to enroll him. "What can you do?" Mr. McLauren asked.

"Well, sir, I can play ball," Nate responded.

Miss Piggy, Mr. Stranger and Mr. McLauren looked at each other crestfallen. If only they had not had to discontinue their sports program just last year. "What else can you do?"

Nate smiled proudly. "I can sing."

Mr. McLauren took him directly to meet Miss Mary Keys, the music teacher. She auditioned him and she and Mr. McLauren gave him a scholarship right on the spot. At Miss Piggy's urging, Mr. McLauren also offered him a work-study program and a stipend for doing odd jobs and janitorial work around campus. Nate's college and lodging would cost him nothing.

It was a dream come true and he was determined not to waste it and not to disappoint Miss Piggy, who had been more kind and helpful to him than anyone in his own family.

Chapter Twenty-one

In a few weeks Nate would return to start classes at Coahoma, but until then helped Mama on the plantation. It was work he had grown to despise just as he despised Mr. Charlie, the master of the plantation. Over the years, Mr. Charlie's disposition had only gotten more bitter, surly and angry. Miss Pat once whispered to Nate, "The good Lord give him the same misery he give to others." Indeed, he had never recovered from the death of his son Elm. "He done blamin' us still for Elm," Miss Pat said. Nate reckoned the old gossip was probably correct. These days though, Mr. Charlie was less of a source of anger for Nate. Still convinced that Nate was crazy, the boss man deliberately stayed away from him. Soon Nate would leave the plantation behind forever. Mr. Charlie was just a distraction for him now.

Still deep down Nate was unhappy. He'd stopped having his night terrors years before, but now it seemed the terror was with him constantly. Sometimes, without warning, he would vividly remember the physical and emotional abuse he suffered. It seemed he was taken back in time to the moments when the abuse occurred. He could hear the crack of the switch slapping his back and feel the pain as it struck his already tender flesh. Unconsciously, as he relived the scene, he would find himself biting his lower lip to keep from screaming or crying out just like he did back then.

Life was so different for him now. No one would dare try to whip him; he was a grown man. He was soon going to greet his new life away from the plantation. Nate could not understand why he still felt so bad. It seemed the closer he got to his dreams, the worse he felt inside. He didn't know why, but he knew he didn't want to feel that way.

Drugs and alcohol became more and more a part of his life. He popped Big Mama's pills and washed them down with liquor. Teenie had marijuana, and Nate began to steal little bits of his stash. As time went on Nate would take just about anything he could get his hands on just so he wouldn't feel his pain. Very few people, if any, knew the extent of Nate's dependence on drugs and alcohol. He kept to himself, never let the substance use interfere with work or school, and never appeared to be drunk or high. Nate was sure he had it under control. He would soon find out how wrong he was.

Big Mama's health was deteriorating. After coming in from the fields, Nate would help Mama care for his grandmother. She couldn't walk anymore and her speech was getting more slurred. Throughout her life she had never taken good care of herself. Her diet was poor, and she almost never saw a doctor. It seemed to Nate that her body was wasting away from years of mismanagement of her health. In spite her mistreatment of him, Nate felt sorry for her. Her husband had left her; she had no visitors coming by to see her. She was truly alone except for her daughter, whom she had so badly abused emotionally throughout her life.

Shortly before Nate was ready to go to Coahoma at Clarksdake, Big Mama passed away in her sleep, presumably from another stroke. The funeral was held at Guiding Star church in Chatham with Reverend Winfield officiating. Only about fifteen or so came to pay their respects. Quite a contrast with her sister's very well attended service.

Mama, of course, was devastated. She loved her mother more than anyone. Without her, Mama didn't know how to handle her own life, how to make decisions for herself. Big Mama always told Mama what to do, what to say, and what to think and feel. When Mama made a mistake, Big Mama was always there to tell her what had been done wrong and then some. Who would help her now?

Under these circumstances, it was especially difficult for Nate to leave Mama and go off to college. His brothers didn't come around much and made it clear they weren't going to take care of

Mama. In fact, it was Mama who took care of them even though they were grown. She bailed them out of jail, lied to cover up their transgressions, and worried and fretted over their actions. Nate was the only person she could count on. The move would be painful. Nate thought to himself, "Big Mama got me one last time with her final act of dying.

A week later Nate left for college. Mama cried and cried and he cried with her, but nothing would stop him. Not even Big Mama's death.

Nate's life began to look more and more promising during the time he was at Coahoma. Dean Debro took a special interest in Nate and thrust him into a leadership role. Although Nate at first was reluctant, he began to grow more comfortable in social settings and spent less time alone than he had for most of his life.

The days were busy and productive. He had his classes and homework, work-study duties, and chorus rehearsals. One day, he told Miss Piggy about the money he'd made cutting hair. She immediately introduced him to Mr. Wellerton who had the local barbershop. Mr. Wellerton soon invited Nate to cut hair in his shop, which brought in a lot of new business in the form of college students. Nate was making more money than ever, and he made sure he took care of Mama, sending her cash each week in a brown envelope. She was the richest sharecropper on Mr. Charlie's plantation. Still she worried and wondered where Nate really got the money and how long his good fortune would last. Part of her believed that Nate had stolen the money.

The first semester passed quickly. Nate was doing very well at school, and he had the constant support and counsel of Miss Piggy to ensure his success. On the weekends, he stayed at her home, and she cooked many wonderful meals for him. In his whole life Nate had never eaten so well. Nate returned her hospitality by cleaning and doing odd jobs around the house. Miss Piggy told him he didn't have to feel beholden to her and certainly did not have to work while he was her guest, but working was Nate's most comfortable state. It dulled his pain almost as much as alcohol or drugs. If he was busy, the bad thoughts could not catch up with him.

In the spring of 1968, Clarksdale was abuzz with excitement.

Dr. Martin Luther King had scheduled a stop there on his way to Memphis to lend support to a strike by sanitation workers in the city. Nate had watched on television with Miss Piggy as Dr. King delivered his "I Have a Dream" speech from the steps of the Capitol in Washington, D. C. Nate was so looking forward to seeing such a great man in person.

And the great man did not disappoint. His presence was breathtaking and his intelligence and character were remarkable. Dr. King met with Miss Piggy, Mr. Arron Henry, Mr. Stranger and several students and faculty, including Nate. He was soft spoken as he talked of the struggles and victories of his campaign for equality. He looked toward the future with optimism and hope. Nate was very moved by Dr. King's words and enthusiasm, as was everyone who listened that day. Dr. King left a lasting impression on Clarksdale.

But their zeal was short-lived. Not long after Dr. King's visit came the heartbreaking news that he had been assassinated in Memphis, Tennessee outside his hotel room. The gunman was James Earl Ray, a white man. A burning rage swept over the campus like a firestorm. One of the dean's other student assistants, Jamison Davis ran up to Nate, who was on his way back to his dorm after finishing his work-study duties. "Have you heard about Dr. King?" Jamison cried blinking back hot angry tears.

Nate stopped. "I can't believe it," he told his friend. "I just can't believe it." Thanks to a few of Big Mama's pills his own rage was muted. Tut Johnson ran up and threw his arms around Nate and Jamison, making no effort to hide his tears. "They killed him," he cried. "Whitey killed him."

The campus was suddenly alive with students. They had come out of their rooms and classes, walking blindly through the campus, not thinking straight, overcome with grief and anger. One young man jumped up on a four-foot wall by the administration building and shouted to the assembling crowd. "Are we gonna left them get away with this? I say no. I say we should take to the streets and take our revenge." The mass of voices shouted in agreement.

Nate felt a tap on his shoulder. It was John Lofton, another of the student assistants. He shouted in Nate's ear over the noise of the crowd. "Dean Debro wants to see us all in his office right away." Nate, Tut, Jamison, and John ran as fast as they could to the Dean's office.

When they arrived the Dean was seated behind his desk his chair turned toward the window where he watched the brewing riot. He turned around and asked his young campus leaders to gather around. "Today is the saddest day I've ever known," he said. Several of the assistants voiced their agreement. Dean Debro stood up. "But we must not let it become even worse. We must not resort to violence. That is not what Dr. King would have wanted."

Tut Johnson was dismayed by his words. "But they killed him in cold blood. They murdered him."

Dean Debro walked over to Tut and put his hands on his shoulders. "Yes, son, a man did murder Dr. King, and he will pay for his crime."

"But Dean," Tut cried, "we gotta stand up for Dr. King. We gotta show whitey that we aren't going to take this."

The Dean stepped back. "And how would you do this? By rioting, by burning our campus, by destroying our town. What would that do but leave us with less than we already have?"

"You're right," Tut said.

"But what should we do?" Nate asked.

The dean walked back to his desk and sat down. "We should carry Dr. King's vision forward. We should refrain from violence and resist oppression through the non-violent means. Dr. King told us about this only days ago in this very room."

Nodding in agreement, the young men suddenly felt empowered as though Dr. King himself had given them charge to carry out his mission, for they had been so fortunate to meet him and hear his counsel.

"I want you all to go out on campus and talk to as many students as you can," the dean told them. "Remind them of Dr. King's vision and our duty to carry it out now that he is gone. Tell them not to destroy the gains we have already made, to leave our campus intact so we can learn to become the leaders of the future because we are the future of our nation and our race."

The young men stood in awe of their Dean and in awe of the

task he had laid out for them. Nate knew Dean Debro was right. Dr. King would not want them to fight and riot. The group turned as one and circulated around the campus. Nate talked to so many people that day he lost count, but at the end of the day he felt invigorated and infused with Dr. King's message. As he persuaded one angry soul after another to stop the desire for vengeance and replace it with a need to move Dr. King's work forward, he realized he had a talent for influencing people. He remembered his longtime wish to use his words and intelligence to help people and change their lives for the better. For the first time he had seen that wish manifest. He could help people change for the better, and he was good at it.

As evening fell that awful night, the campus had calmed down considerably. There were only one or two small violent but isolated outbursts. No rioting or destruction would take place on the campus of Coahoma.

Chapter Twenty-two

In the aftermath of the assassination of Dr. King and the student assistants' intervention, the students of Coahoma calmed and returned to their studies. Although he was proud of his role in averting disaster at school, Nate struggled with his own anger. The death of Dr. King at the hands of a white man caused Nate's rage to resurface. Night after night he awoke from nightmares of Mr. Charlie taunting him. "You don't need to go to school to pick cotton," a ghostly boss man shouted at him. "You aint never gonna amount to nothin', you crazy little son of a bitch." One night he woke at 3 AM screaming. In his dream, he had been chased and beaten by a posse of plantation men, who threw him unconscious into a pig trough. As he awoke, the animals were nuzzling the skin of his face, getting ready to feed on his flesh.

"Nate, what the hell's the matter," whispered his roommate Charles Davis, whom everyone called Sugar Bear. He was standing over Nate, who lay shaking in his bed.

Nate sat up, rubbed his eyes and grabbed his friend's arm. "A bad dream," he said, "a really bad dream. I'll be all right. Go back to sleep. " He threw his legs over the side of the bed while Sugar Bear sat down on the floor in front of him.

"Tell me about it," Sugar Bear said.

"Nah," Nate answered, "go on back to bed. You need your rest. I'll be all right."

Sugar Bear turned on the lamp. "No, man, you need to tell me about it, and I aint takin' no for an answer."

As he looked into Sugar Bear's eyes, Nate realized he was serious. Unaccustomed to sharing about himself, Nate felt very uncomfortable, but he knew he had to speak. Reluctantly he began to tell Sugar Bear about his dream and the real life situations that had inspired it. Before he knew it Nate was telling him all about his childhood and the deprivation he had endured. He told him all about the beatings at the hands of Mama, Big Mama, CW, and Teenie, even sharing his hiding place of the chimney hole under the house. Story after story poured out of him. He cried when he spoke of having so little to wear he had to wash out his clothes, ragged and tattered, every evening so he'd have something to put on everyday. His shoes, explained were glued together over and over so he'd have something to cover his feet.

As the sun began to rise over the administration building, Nate was still talking. Sugar Bear listened patiently, and only interjected here and there to ask a question or to say, "That must have been painful," or "That must have been hard." Nate was amazed by his friend's lack of judgment and comforting empathy. "Look outside," Nate said, "it's morning already and we aint got no sleep."

Sugar Bear smiled. "That's okay. This was more important."

Nate smiled back at his friend. Sugar Bear was right. Nate felt like a weight had been lifted from his heart.

"But," Sugar Bear added, "we can catch a couple hours before class. I'm goin' back to bed."

Nate lay down on his bed and as he drifted off to sleep he thanked God for the friendship of his roommate. Sugar Bear was a big young man, quite a bit over weight, and many of his classmates made fun of him. Nate felt fortunate to know Sugar Bear's patient, tender heart that lay beneath the outer appearance that others ridiculed.

Several weeks later Nate became ill with a bad flu. He was confined to his bed and unable to attend his classes or work cutting hair. As he lay ailing he worried that he would not be able to send any money home to Mama. He fretted over how Mama would survive without his extra funds. At one point he tried to get out of bed to head down to Mr. Wellerton's shop to work, but he collapsed in a spasm of coughing. Sugar Bear ran over and helped him back into bed. "You aint goin' nowhere," Sugar Bear said, sounding as strong and firm as Nate had ever heard him. Nate was too weak to argue.

Still he tried. "But I got to go work," he said. "I need to make some money to take care of Mama."

"Don't you worry about nothin'," Sugar Bear told him. "I'll take care of things." With that he left, and Nate fell fast asleep.

When Sugar Bear returned, Nate awoke bleary eyed. "Here you go," Sugar Bear said handing Nate a fat envelope.

"What's this?" Nate opened the flap to find it filled with cash. "Sugar Bear, what's this?"

"It's for your Mama," he said.

"But I can't take this money. It belongs to you."

"It's for your Mama. And I don't want to hear no more. You get some rest now."

Nate stared at him in disbelief, but he knew Sugar Bear was serious. "Thank you, man," he said with tears welling up in his eyes. "Thank you."

When he felt better Nate sent the money to Mama. He never knew where or how Sugar Bear had gotten it, but he was sure he had never had a more true and loyal friend.

Before he knew it Nate's second year at Coahoma had begun and it was already Thanksgiving break. He returned to the plantation to see Mama and spend the holiday with her. While he was there he saw a young lady he had been dating for the past four years. The two had dated, but had never been intimate. That was to change during his few days home. On a cold November evening the pair had sex. It was the first time for both.

Nate returned to school; spending the Christmas holidays on campus, he agreed to watch Dean Debro's home while he was away. Nate enjoyed the trust and responsibility he was given on campus. His professors liked him, he was popular among the students, and his grades were good. For the first time in his life he felt important, like he was somebody. He was moving forward toward the life he had dreamed about all his life. He began to feel that he would major in psychology when he transferred from junior college to a university. He wanted to become a psychologist to help others with their problems. His goal it seemed was well within his grasp.

But fate would deal him a test. Life would not be that easy for him. In January, he received a letter from his young lady back on the plantation. He was excited to hear from her. It had been a few weeks since she had written. Tearing open the letter, he began to read. But the news was not good. She wrote that she had not gotten her period since they had sex, and she believed she might be pregnant with his child.

Nate saw all his dreams begin to crumble. How could he support a wife and a child and his Mama and still continue with school? There was no question he would marry her. Folks on the plantation viewed him now as a responsible man, a far cry from the crazy boy they had gossiped about when he was a child. Miss Pat and Miss Chaney had long said to their circle of hens, "Look at how he takes care of his Mama, whoever he marries will never have to worry about nothin'."

By March it was clear, his young lady was pregnant. When he returned to the plantation for a spring break visit, Nate told his mother and brothers that he would marry his expectant girlfriend as soon as he finished school.

When he returned to classes, Nate worked harder than ever. He needed to keep his grades up, but he also had to make more money. Now he had two women and soon a child to support. In the evenings and on weekends he cut so many heads of hair he developed blisters on his thumb and index fingers where the scissors rested. Week after week two envelopes of money left the town post bound for Mama and his young bride to be.

The remainder of his time at Coahoma went by in a rush or so it felt to Nate. It seemed life was moving too fast, like his dreams were passing him by once again. He graduated in mid-June and celebrated alone with a handful of pills and a bottle of cheap whiskey. Duty was ruling his life. After a few sips of liquor, it didn't seem quite so bad.

On June 17 at 1 PM he married the mother of his nearly one-year-old daughter. His wife's uncle Verline stood up for them at the courthouse and was the only other person in attendance. His wife was happy, nearly breathless with joy as they said their vows. Nate's mind was elsewhere. He had a wife and child. He needed to provide for them. Mama wanted him to come back to the plantation, and his wife's family seemed to agree, but for Nate that was not an option.

At 2 PM after the brief exchanging of vows, Nate boarded a Trailways bus with an attaché case that contained a pair of pants, a shirt, a couple of pairs of under shorts, and his hair clippers. He had only five dollars in his pocket. He was bound for St. Louis where he had some friends who had agreed to let him stay with them until he got established. Reluctantly, he left his wife and daughter in the charge of her uncle who would return her to her family. She wanted very much to go along with her husband, but Nate said no unequivocally. He would send for her when he had a place for them to live.

As he sat on the cold bus, Nate was consumed with worry. He recalled his wife's innocent face as she looked up at him at the station. He promised her she would be with him soon. She was so trusting and so much in love with him, and she believed in him. "Don't worry," Nate told her. "We'll all be together before you know it."

Nate looked out the window and watched the world outside flying by. He didn't know what he would do once he got to St. Louis. He didn't know how he would earn enough money to support Mama and his wife and child. He didn't know if he would ever go back to school and become the doctor of psychology he dreamed of being. He didn't know if he would ever send for his young family. Would he be a good husband and father? He didn't know anything.

Chapter Twenty-three

Although he carried only five dollars with him on his trip to St. Louis, Nate had more money. True to form Nate sacrificed and denied himself to provide for others. The rest of his money had been given to his wife and Mama. He would do without so that the three women in his life had food and clothing.

When he got to St. Louis, Nate would be staying with Mac and his wife Wedia, who had moved there at Wedia's Uncle Tom's insistence a couple of years ago. Mac was a childhood friend from the plantation, and Wedia's aunt was married to Nate's brother. The couple was practically family and had extended their home to Nate while he got on his feet in the new city. "You call me when you get here," Mac told him during a phone conversation. "I'll come down and get you. You hear." Knowing his friend's reluctance to accept help, Mac made Nate promise to call the minute he got off the arrived.

The bus pulled into the St. Louis bus depot at 10:45 PM, and Nate decided to vacate his promise. It was too late to call. He didn't want to disturb his friends at such a late hour. Making his way out to the street, he hailed a cab. The driver was a crotchety old man, who complained about the city the entire ride. The taxes were too high, the crime rate soaring, and jobs getting more and more scarce. Nate slumped in his seat. This was certainly not the welcome he had hoped for. When he'd been to St. Louis in the past, it seemed like a beautiful, hopeful, bustling place. So unlike where he grew up, seemingly so full of opportunity. He was quite dismayed to hear the cab driver's spiel. Yet it all fit in with how his life was going.

When the cab reached Mac's house, the meter read $5.25.

Twenty-five cents plus tip more than Nate had. "Look, man, I only got a five," Nate said, "but you give me your number and I'll get the rest to you soon as I can."

The driver turned around and faced his fare. At the end of a long hard night of driving around the city he was about to scream at yet another dead beat, but then he saw the look in Nate's eyes. He somehow could see he could trust this man. "Nah, go on," he said, "Don't worry about it. Take care of yourself and good luck."

Nate thanked him and got out of the cab. He stood on the sidewalk for a few minutes watching the cab drive down the street. Then he knocked on the door of Mac's old red brick row house. Wedia answered and quickly ushered him inside. "Nate you look awful," she scolded. "Come on inside."

"I'm all right," Nate said as Wedia tugged him into the house by his arm. Mac rushed up to greet him with a big hug.

"So good to see you," he told his friend. "It's been too long."

After talking for only a couple of minutes, Mac and Wedia went off to bed. Mac had to be up early for his job at Barnes hospital. Nate bedded down on the couch, sleeping with his clothes on. He was exhausted and fell asleep quickly.

In the morning Nate assured his friends he would not be any trouble, he would take care of himself, and would be gone as soon as he got a job and enough money to rent a room. Mac told Nate he could stay as long as he needed. Wedia laughed and said, "Sure as I'm standin' if I knows anything I know you won't be puttin' us out. Anyone else, yeah, but you never."

Nate splashed some water on his face, and headed out on foot to look for a job. He spent all day going from one business to another, but had no luck. The next day he did the same with the same result. His welcome to St. Louis seminar courtesy of the old cabbie was more accurate than he'd realized. Jobs were scarce, the economy was worse, and things were not looking promising for his new life in St. Louis. Nate tried to keep from panicking. His wife and daughter and his mother were depending on him. Had he made a big mistake coming to this strange city? Would he have been better off listening to Mama and his wife's family and staying on the plantation?

At the end of the hot, humid second day of searching for work he dragged himself back to Mac's house exhausted and dejected. He sat on the porch and waited until Mac returned from the hospital. Nate told Mac he couldn't find a job. Mac wasn't surprised, knowing times were tough in the city. He encouraged his friend to keep trying.

"Oh, I'm not gonna quit," Nate assured him, "but meantime if you don't mind, I can cut hair here."

"Nah, don't mind at all," Mac said. "just be sure and clean up real good or Wedia will come after us both with a broom, and she won't be sweepin'."

The two men laughed together. It felt good to laugh again Nate thought to himself. It seemed like it had been a long time.

"Why don't you ask the men at the hospital if any of them wants a good hair cut for 50 cents?"

"I sure will."

It wasn't long before men from the hospital and their friends and family were coming by Mac's house to get haircuts. Once again, Nate reputation spread quickly and soon his business was booming. He made a tidy bit of money after a week, but he turned it over to his hosts. They protested a bit, not wanting to keep him from taking care of his own, but Nate assured them he wouldn't feel right staying another day if he didn't repay them for their hospitality.

Nate continued to cut hair for the next several weeks quite successfully. One Saturday a line stretched from Mac's front door a half block to the corner. A foot patrolman walking by saw the gathering and followed the line up to the front door. He knocked to find out what was going on and was rather relieved to find out the benign reason for the assemblage. Whenever he didn't have heads to trim, Nate looked for a job and was disappointed time and time again. Haircutting afforded him enough money to send home to his wife and Mama, but he knew he would not make enough to move his family to the city just by cutting hair.

As the days passed Nate became more and more frustrated. He began to go out in the evenings because he didn't feel right hanging around Mac's house. Soon he had found the drinking and drugging crowd. He began to drink every night and experiment with drugs like tranquilizers, cocaine and even heroin. For awhile he was still able to get up in the morning and continue to search for a job and return to cut hair in the afternoons, but soon he started having trouble getting up in the morning. He began to hate himself, to hate the way he was living, the budding failure he had become. Each night the drugs and booze made him feel a little better, but every morning he felt worse and worse.

One day as he made his daily trek to find work, he passed by some men standing together on a street corner. The tall one a thin, dark skinned man about ten years older than Nate approached him. "Hey, man, take a hit off this," he said. "It's prime shit, man. Best in the city."

Nate stared at the marijuana cigarette in front of his face, and with little hesitation took a long drag and held it in. His lungs burned from the smoke as he exhaled, but he was almost instantly high. "He aint lyin'" Nate thought. "This is good shit." He remembered from time to time smoking some of Teenie's weed, but that stuff never got him feeling so good as this variety the street peddler was pushing.

The look of pleasant surprise on Nate's face as the smoke left his lips struck the group funny, and all burst out laughing. Nate laughed, too, but was a bit embarrassed.

"You all right, man," said the tall one. "Tell you what I'm gonna do." He rubbed his chin then reached out and touched Nate's shoulder. "I gots some I can sell you cheap if you's interested."

"How much?" Nate asked.

"I gots me five joints. I can give 'em to you for two sawbucks."

Nate hesitated. That would seriously cut into the money he was going to send to Mama and his wife and the cash he was trying to save to get his own place for his family.

The tall one passed the joint to him again. "Here," he said, "have another hit. This shit is fine. I'm offering you a deal, man."

Nate took another drag off the joint and suddenly twenty dollars didn't seem like that much. "Okay, man," he said. "I'll take 'em." He pulled the money out of his pocket and stuffed the joints into his jacket.

"That's cool, man," said the tall one. "That's cool."

Nate turned to walk away, but the tall one stopped him. "Hey, man, why don't you stick around and finish this one?"

Nate obliged and they finished the joint and lit another. By that time Nate was feeling very good. His troubles had melted away. He chatted and laughed with the street corner men for a couple of hours before he took his leave. They made him promise to come back and hang out with them again soon, but Nate would never return and he knew it. He would rather do his drinking and drugging alone and always had.

The next morning after Mac and Wedia had left for the day Nate sunk into a deep depression. He couldn't find a job in spite of all his efforts. He saw himself as a failure—a failure as a man, as a husband, as a father. His dream of going back to school seemed to have died. Worst of all, he began to believe that Mr. Charlie was right. Nate Lowe, the crazy child in a man's body, would never amount to anything. He was doomed to fail from birth. He cursed himself for ever even trying to be something. The fruitless efforts at success and education seemed embarrassing. He imagined the gossip on the plantation, the smug look on Mr. Charlie's face when he heard of the crazy boy's failure. His only comfort was that Big Mama was not alive to see it. Her ridicule would have been more than he could bear.

Above all Nate doubted himself. How could he possibly be a good father to his child and a good husband to his wife when he had no one to show him how? His father had abandoned him and his mother and had no presence in his life. Nate had no idea how to be a man because no one had showed him how. Miss Pat and her hens were wrong. Nate could never be the man they said he would. He had no idea how to do it. Although it was only nine in the morning, Nate went outside and pulled a bottle of Morgan Davis wine from behind a bush where he had hidden it. By noon he had drunk the bottle and smoked two of the joints he had bought. There would be no job hunting that day.

One evening as he alone sat in a dive bar downtown, Nate caught his reflection in the beveled mirror behind the bartender. He cursed himself and his lot in life. He thought about his father. An almost ghostlike figure behind a pair of black framed sunglasses.

He knew so little about him. Robbed of the wisdom a father passes to his son, Nate reasoned he had no idea how to be a man. Even if he had been in Nate's life and had been a bad father, at least he would have known how not to be. He left Nate with nothing. Nathaniel Sr. was just a dark shadow for his son and a heartbreak for Mama. Tears welled up in Nate's eyes. "Will I be a shadow and heartbreak to my child and wife," he thought.

As he sipped a glass of Jack on the rocks, he began to question whether or not he wanted to live. He put his head in his hands and a tear fell from his eye as he answered, "No." He did not want to live. No longer did he want to be a failure. No longer did he want to live out the curse of his existence. Suddenly he felt resigned yet purposeful. He knew what he had to do.

The next day after cutting twenty heads of hair, he skipped his usual foot search for a job and instead went to a local pawnshop on the corner of Delmar and DeBolivar Blvd. In a rare instance of spending his money on himself, he bought a .22 revolver and some bullets. It was plain, no frills, black metal, but it would do the job.

The next morning he cut a few more heads. He sealed the remainder of his money into two envelopes—one for his wife, the other for Mama—and mailed what he thought would be his last offerings to his family back on the plantation. He packed his attaché case, and loaded his gun and shut it inside the case.

Feeling hung-over and tired he walked downtown to the park. It was a cloudy Tuesday and the park was nearly deserted, and he was glad. He didn't want his final act to disturb anyone. Trudging through the freshly mown grass, he approached the great silver arch of St. Louis and sat down in the middle of its grand arc. No one was around, and it was peaceful and open and free.

Purposefully, he took the gun out of the attaché case and took out all but one, lone bullet. He spun the chamber and held the gun to his head. "God, please forgive me," he whispered aloud. "I don't know why my life is cursed, but I just can't take it no more. I'm so sorry. Please take care of the people I leave behind. I just can't do it no more." Suddenly he felt s sense of calmness. He looked up to the sky, placed the gun to his temple and pulled the trigger. He heard the click and waited. But nothing happened.

"God damn me," he shouted, "I can't even get this right." Angrily, he opened up the gun. Sure enough there was the bullet unspent. Furious, he spun the chamber around again. "Just let me get this right, Lord. Just let me get this right." In an instant he put the gun to his head and pulled the trigger. Nothing.

He dropped the gun and collapsed to the grass in tears. "Why? Why?" he sobbed. A strong gust of wind blew over his convulsing body, ruffling the collar of his only shirt. The air was warm and he suddenly began to feel warm inside There was a feeling of strength and relief that penetrated to the core of him, and he suddenly realized he had gotten it right. God had a plan for him. There was a reason the bullet did not fire into his head. He was supposed to live. He was supposed to succeed. This failure, this colossal failure would be his last. He took the gun and threw it into the Mississippi River down from the arch.

The very next day Nate went out and finally he found a job at a printing shop that made the stars that appeared on the back of water heaters. The shop owner told him, "If you're a quick learner, I'll show you the business." On his off hours he continued to cut hair, moving to the back porch so as not to inconvenience Wedia. He saved every penny so he could get a place of his own. Making about $85 a week at his job and the same amount cutting hair, he soon got a small, furnished apartment.

Of all the revelations he'd had after his suicide attempt, one stood out most clearly—he would never again use drugs or alcohol. He had spent a big part of his life in an alcohol and drug induced daze to dull the pain of his childhood, but that had to end. God had a plan for Nate Lowe, and he had to be clear headed to carry out His plan.

In August 1968 he went back to the plantation and brought his wife and child to live with him. Over the years he would have three more daughters, and he remained determined that they would know their father. He wanted them to understand that in spite of how hard his life had been he was determined to make their lives better. To accomplish this goal he went on with his education, buying his first home while still in graduate school. Eventually he earned his PhD in psychology and has worked in that professional field to this day.

In 1970 he moved Mama off the plantation and set her up in an apartment in St. Louis. She was scared at first and reluctant to leave the only life she had ever known, but Nate took care of her, made sure she had money and whatever she needed for the rest of her life. When Nate and his family moved from St. Louis to pursue his education, she stayed on having created a comfortable life with friends and family in her new city.

Chapter Twenty-four

The call came on a rainy December night in 2002. Nate's cell phone rang as he was driving home from his work as the head of substance abuse prevention programs for the United States Marine Corps at Miramar, San Diego, California. He immediately recognized the number as coming from Mississippi, and he answered instead of letting it go to voicemail as he frequently did. A man much in demand to help others in need of psychological counseling and crisis intervention, Nate frequently did not have enough hours in the day to do all the counseling he was called upon to do. But this call was from one of his brothers, and his brothers didn't call unless it was important.

The voice on the line was James his youngest brother, who had grown to be the most social of his clan. Still James only called but a few times a year, and although Nate was happy to hear from him, he sensed something was wrong.

"I gots some bad news," James said.

"Lay it on me," said Nate. He was quite accustomed to listening to the trials and tribulations of many through his work, but when it was family, it was impossible to be the detached, professional doctor-therapist.

"It's me. The doc say I got cancer."

"Oh no…" Nate's mind raced to memories of his younger brother, the ladies man, the life of the party. He always somehow wriggled out of the stickiest of situations, but also had his share of struggles with the law and with drugs and alcohol, but he had turned his life around. "And it all comes down to this," Nate thought as he drove down the freeway on ramp. "So funny how life is."

"I need to see you," James told him.

Without hesitation, Nate replied, "I'll be there as soon as I can."

It took him a few days to arrange time off, but by the end of the week he was on the road headed for Hattiesburg, Mississippi about four hours from Lake Jackson where the four boys, known on the plantation as the Willie B boys, grew up. Nate avoided flying, favoring instead long drives alone. He liked the solitude and felt he did his best thinking on the road. And there was the freedom from work, which he had done, non-stop throughout his entire life, often working three jobs and seeing patients on the side.

He knew he could make it from California to Mississippi in a few days driving straight through covering 700 miles each day. He started his trek at five am and drove until 10 pm on the southern route over I-10. He stopped at a lonely truck stop, grabbed a bite to eat and then slept in his car. As dawn broke he awoke got some breakfast, washed up in the restroom, and then hit the road again.

By mid-day, he hit a bad rainstorm. The rain was so heavy he could barely see the road. He began to pray aloud, "Lord please take care of me. If it's my time, I'm ready to go, but if it isn't, please protect me." As soon as he had finished uttering his entreaty to God, the rain stopped. Nate felt goose bumps on his forearm, and tears formed in his eyes. As the dry road, whizzed under his wheels, he thanked God for His protection. This was not the first time God had intervened in his life and saved him, and he hoped it would not be the last. The massive heart attack and quadruple bypass surgery of five years ago was just the latest example. Few survived such an ordeal, and even fewer with their strength and mental capacities completely intact.

A wave of guilt suddenly washed over him. God had never let him down. In fact, he frequently told many souls in their times of need, "God did not bring you this far to leave you." But he had left God. When he was a boy and younger man, he had been so involved in church, and he enjoyed an active spiritual life. As he got older, the demand of his work began to take precedence and he had gotten farther and farther away from his spirituality. Still as he had just seen, God had never left him.

As he drove onward on the Interstate, he regretted his distance from his God. He vowed that when he returned home he would work hard to change that.

After another night's sleep at a truck stop, he was back on the road. His destination now was within imagining, and he began to settle into the drive with a sense of peace and calmness. He reflected on his brothers and his difficult childhood—-making a concerted effort to prevent his thoughts from dwelling on the negative experiences of that time so long ago. He tried very hard to keep the bad memories out of his consciousness, wanting instead to remember the good times he shared with his brothers.

But no matter how hard he tried the dark thoughts broke through. There was Mama standing before him cursing him for no reason at all except that she'd had a bad day. "I hate the day you were born," she shouted with a look of hatred that made him shiver. As soon as he'd banished that from his mind, a vision of Teenie laughing, coming after him with a pine switch, "Boy, I gonna whoop you so bad." And there was James telling Mama and CW, Nate had smacked him when it was really James who'd bitten Nate. And the beating CW delivered for that one...

But that was so long ago, Nate told himself. So many years and so many accomplishments ago. Life had been tough for all the Willie B Boys. Each of them did what they had to do to survive, and each of them did survive. That was what mattered now.

God had gotten them through and He had always sent Nate just the right person at just the right time to help him. As he drove, Nate reflected on those souls who had helped him make it through his awful childhood. There were his teachers Miss Miller and Miss Vaughn, and Mr. Redmond and Mr. Williams. On the plantation he had Ma Pearl, Mr. Sylvester, and Mathilda Griffin and his invaluable friend Chip. And later in his life he'd been sent Miss Piggy, Dean Debro and his true friend Sugar Bear. Each made a great difference in his life and each played a part in Nate getting off the plantation. Each was instrumental in his or her own way in Nate becoming the successful man he dreamed he'd be as he picked cotton hour after hour day after day in the hot Mississippi sun.

When he arrived in Hattiesburg he went to the west side first where James lived. His youngest brother was overjoyed to see him and the two embraced. James was a little wobbly with his right foot in a cast. He'd broken it while playing ball with his children. James led Nate proudly through his modest home, which was comfortably furnished and neat and clean.

The two brothers sat down across from each other in the living room and James' wife brought them lemonade. As they talked Nate realized how proud he was of James. He was a caring and sensitive man with a strong sense of family. James reached over and touched his brother's arm and told him how important it was that they got together at this time. "We don't have our parents no more," he said. "We're all we got. We need to be there for each other."

James' wisdom was born of many hard years of overcoming addiction. He also suffered an injury to his back while working in a steel mill. The ruptured disk made it impossible for him to work and left him in constant pain. James, too, had endured a childhood with an absent father, and later in life when he found his father again, he was devastated when the man he had idolized but barely knew rejected him. It was a pain Nate knew all too well.

After a half hour or so the brothers drove to Teenie's house on the east side. They went inside and greeted their oldest brother now 73. He answered them with a voice that was much weaker than Nate had expected.

Nate reached out and hugged Teenie. He still looked much the same but for a hint of gray in his hair. Nate marveled that Teenie was looking so much like his beloved Mama, the same eyes, nose and wide forehead. It was almost like seeing her again.

Teenie had struggled for decades with addiction and brushes with the law, but with the help of his second wife he had overcome his addiction. Once clean and sober he felt his calling to become a minister. Now retired, Teenie ministered to hundreds of souls and left behind a thriving congregation that drew inspiration and comfort from his heartfelt sermons every Sunday.

For hours the brothers talked and laughed and reminisced. When Nate announced it was time for him to go, Teenie led them in a prayer of thanks for their reunion as the brothers bowed their heads. A man with a strong spiritual connection, Teenie asked God to bless them and keep each one in his care. As he got up to leave Teenie reached out and took Nate's hand and shook it strongly. Nate saw pride in his older brother's eyes as he looked into his.

James embraced Nate. "Thanks, brother," James said his voice cracking with emotion. "Thank you for coming all this way. It mean so much. It give me strength."

Nate stepped back. "Of course I had to come," he said. "You're my baby brother, but not such a baby anymore." The three brothers laughed. And there was something Nate saw in James—a spark that had not been there before. It was then Nate knew James beat his cancer.

Plantation life was hard and unfair, but the brothers survived, and it made them tough and resilient. The poison of drugs and alcohol nearly ruined each of them, but they were clean and sober and now knew true serenity and faith. The Willie B boys were strong and together and with God's help they would overcome anything.

Printed in the United States
69450LVS00004B/1-153